Slamma Lamma Ding Dong

D1372924

Slamma Lamma Ding Dong

An Anthology by Nebraska's Slam Poets

JM Huscher, Matt Mason, Dan Leamen
editors

iUniverse, Inc.
New York Lincoln Shanghai

Slamma Lamma Ding Dong
An Anthology by Nebraska's Slam Poets

iUniverse books may be ordered through booksellers or by contacting:

iUniverse
2021 Pine Lake Road, Suite 100
Lincoln, NE 68512
www.iuniverse.com
1-800-Authors (1-800-288-4677)

ISBN-13: 978-0-595-36297-4 (pbk)
ISBN-13: 978-0-595-80737-6 (ebk)
ISBN-10: 0-595-36297-4 (pbk)
ISBN-10: 0-595-80737-2 (ebk)

Printed in the United States of America

Contents

Foreword . . . . *vii*

Bad Andy *1*

Ayanna Boykins *6*

Sandra Brennan *8*

Keith Brown *11*

JV Brummels *16*

Erica Chu *18*

Nat Derickson *19*

Katie F-S *24*

Brian Finn *30*

Charles Fort *36*

Monica Fuglei *38*

Dominique Garay *40*

Randy Gustafson *44*

Cath Haftings *45*

Elliot Harmon *46*

Heidi Hermanson *53*

Jack Hubbell *56*

JM Huscher *62*

Melissa A. Kandido *69*

Bruce Koborg *71*

Angie Kritenbrink *74*

Dan Leamen *77*

Sara Lihz *82*

Matt Mason *87*

Amy McGeorge *93*

Grizz McIntosh *97*

Sarah McKinstry-Brown *100*

Michele Mitchell *104*

Jim Morrison *106*

Chris Murray *107*

Zedeka Poindexter *114*

Terry lee Schifferns *117*

Jen Shafer *119*

Timothy Siragusa *121*

Mitch Tracy *122*

Foreword

When one thinks of Omaha as a city, or even Nebraska as a state (because Nebraska certainly isn't a city, and we're not even going to bring up counties here), you might not immediately think of poetry or spoken word and its mark on the rest of the country. I know I didn't the first time I learned about the two. I was probably five years old when I first heard of Nebraska. Somehow, only cows and flatness were related to that region. More than say, Boston and Massachusetts. My brain could only correlate milk-y mammals and a lack of hills.

Then in 2003, I met a wonderful man named Matt Mason, who confirmed the imagery I associated with his home state, but also proved to me that there were things happening in the realm of art, poetry and creativity. And they were also good things done well.

In 2004, I made my first visit to Omaha, Nebraska and was introduced to a group of people that had interests in things other than cows and flatness, but loved where they were and were from. Omaha and Nebraska meant a lot to them, but they were tired of the perception the rest of the world had about their home and land. Their people.

The place wasn't dried up. It was very, very moist...and getting moister.

People from all walks of life have things to say. And sometimes, especially in Omaha, it is a place of old, with a thriving vein of youth. Its words and tone are akin to that of a midwest by the sea. A scene on par with that of Seattle or Austin. Worcester and San Jose. It is English learned and it is languange lived. The poets of Nebraska are not copying the poets of New York, they are waiting to be copied. They are ready to influence a world that only looks to the big cities for the next big thing. Nebraska might have it and it may be in this book. Look hard past the cows and the flatness and you will see words like milk rolling down hills of humor, sorrow, grief and madness. Words just like the ones they sell for $10.00 in Los Angeles, only a bit more real.

As of now, when I'm reminded of Nebraska, or asked at random on the street while wearing a cone bra, I can say that I think of its poets and it's words, long before I think of anything else. The poets there are changing the landscape.

This book will be a surprise to you, as it should. A surprise at how it took you this long to think differently about Nebraska.

You should visit more often.

Mike McGee

Bad Andy

Why Professional Wrestling Is Real

It's a little known fact that the first King crowned in Memphis wasn't Elvis or even Jerry Lawler, but a lone star out of Texas…an Amarillo armadillo breaking Gabronnis with bare hands at every carnival contest along the way. A diamond ring Cadillac man scratching the smile from every backstage mirror that greeted his opponents after a match…wrestler SPUTNICK MONROE!

Christened in Alabama by an ancient oracle of a Caucasian woman, she reading his future in her racist outrage at the audacity he displayed entering the whites-only section of her 1950's audience…. his arm around a black friend! Quickly exhausting her limited vocabulary of ammunition as she RAILED against this blasphemy, she mixed her white metaphors with red rage to spit McCarthy at him in Communist Pinko recrimination…" That man's a damn Sputnik!"

He spun into orbit, the ultimate heel bruised against the backbone of a divided politeness. A satellite falling to earth at the birth place of rock n' roll, he shattered onto the scene leaving craters for footprints…strolling down the wrong side of Beale St. in Lansky brothers suites, forcing the cops to arrest him for vagrancy…daring the clerks at Dillard's to eject HIS African comrades for not taking off their hats inside. 220 pounds of twisted steel and sex appeal forcing segregation to take a five minute running head start whenever it saw him coming. He never saw himself as a savior or a white enabler…just a widow's peak forcing stupidity to show the courage of its pointy little convictions.

A bare-chested Buddha holding court in the ring, "Win if you can, lose if you must, always cheat, and if they take you out, leave TEARING DOWN THE RING!" A brawling precursor to the nonviolent freedom riders, he was turned down for a seat for saying that if anyone tried to stop the bus he'd come out with a machine gun. See, he wasn't saved, so he spent every dirty trick he had matching the old south for every fast one it tried to pull on his watch. It was never about trying to get other whites to share what they had, it was about embodying the beer swilling, rippling, ill-tempered, line crossing, leg popping, unapologetic, "I'll Jump In The Air and Shit In Your Hair" FACT that they no longer had a choice.

The lights go down for the main event at the ghost of Ellis Auditorium. The blood fever between sputnik and Billy Wicks has fevered half the county and crowd threatens to burst the place like an aneurism. Hundreds of affordably priced tickets have made their way into every neighborhood 20 miles east of the Mississippi and laid siege to the grand old arena. Sputnik enters the ring and raises his hands…up, over every cracker in the good seats… up, into the Jim Crow's Nest balcony…up, to his real fans. With one voice, the red sea parts for every Bluff City son and daughter in attendance and the color line rolls back like so much surf. White and black mixes together crashing, swirling, screaming for Sputnik or Billy… Integration had gate crashed Memphis, and it was out for blood!

Open letter to the brothers of the book

Hey, Christians, Muslims and Jews
Can I have you're attention, just for a sec?
I admit,
It's been riveting,
On-the-edge-of-my-seat drama
I'm so scared that I want to quit my job
stock up on snack food and wait for the end to come
but I'm not so frightened that I'm not gonna tell you something first:
This is ridiculous
You guys represent three big groups of people

with a lot of things in common
Each of you worships a god that says
"Be nice to people"
Spoke to Moses and said
"I've ten rules that are really gonna make things better…"
Now a rational person might think
"Wow, they all have to be nice to people and
They've agreed on ten basic rules about how to act…
I bet they spend a lot of time helping each other out with that."
Well, it seems the one thing
you've all agreed on
Is taking certain rules off the table completely.
Let's start with the most basic one
"Thou shalt not kill."
Extremely simple concept, and yet
All of you are doing a piss poor job of not killing people
Nobody's getting into heaven, paradise, or the afterlife saying,
"Oooooh, DON'T kill…
Boy, is MY face red."
This is not advanced grammar
Four word sentence…
Underline the subject once, the verb twice
"You…don't kill."
Not only are you not "not killing"
You're actually one-upping each other
At who can come up with the most creative way
To kill the largest number of people at once!
Now, if you believe god said "be nice",
Having to spell out "don't kill" is a little redundant
Because, frankly, not killing someone
Is the first thing you have to do
In order to be nice to them
You get those mixed up and it just doesn't work at all

"Die unbeliever! Oh wait, is there anything I can do to cheer you up?
Hello? Unbeliever? Oh well…
Maybe I should have asked him before riddling him with gunfire"
Now Judaism, and Islam are not my strong points

But, I can forgive them a little confusion
Since both have stories, early on,
That go right from God saying "This is how it is"
To prophets declaring war on people
But the christians?
You guys have absolutely no excuse on this one
Jesus never killed anyone
In fact, this one time in the Bible
Some roman soldiers showed up
With the express purpose of killing HIM
And not only did he not try to kill them or even stop them
But when one of his followers cut a bad guy's ear off
Jesus actually put it back on and then chewed his own follower out…
I think the "no killing" moral of that story
would be obvious to a coma patient
What would Jesus do?
Apparently, he wouldn't kill anyone!
So you've got three major religions
All of them saying "be nice" and "don't kill"
Get them all together wait a few hundred years
And what happens?
A non-killing, be nice love in?
Try muslims killing the christians, the christians killing the muslims
And everyone killing the hell out of the jews
And that was just in the last thousand years or so
Now the jews have bitten off a piece started an army
That kills muslims on a daily basis
The muslims get so mad
that they start randomly killing christians and jews with bombs…
TIME OUT!
You're so badly off the tracks that anyone with half a brain
Has to run for their lives from the whole mess
"Look out! It's the people that love everyone!"
"Run away before they try to be nice to you!"
I'm not saying that somebody's team can't win eventually
But if you don't live like you talk
there may be nobody left for God to come back for
when you're finished

Prayer is...

Right now, Prayer is a pair of 19 year old kids in Baghdad who just want to live through the night, and as long as each doesn't find out where the other one is, they'll both get their wish.

Right now, Prayer is 13 and so desperate that she'll strike a deal with God, Satan or any power who can hear her, if it will just keep her brother in his own bedroom tonight.

Right now, Prayer is just learning how to talk and doesn't yet understand what she's saying. But she knows when Daddy's eyes are closed and his hands are folded together the things he's saying are something the whole family listens to.

Right now, Prayer is just coming to grips with the idea that after 87 years of waking up every morning, he probably won't tomorrow.

Right now, Prayer is 34 and just watched the most important responsibility he's ever agreed to take on open his eyes for the first time and open his mouth to add his voice to the world.

Right now, Prayer is being offered by an enemy like a gift that will never be opened.

Right now, Prayer is as cheap as the talk it's made of.

Right now, Prayer is being remembered just a little too late to be done.

Right now, Prayer is the only company a prisoner has on his 15th day in solitary.

Right now, Prayer is glad just to be able to make the rent this month.

Prayer isn't an audience with the almighty as much as a CAT scan that you know how to read for yourself.

God isn't dead, He's just listening…waiting…not for you to tell him what you want. He already knows that. He just doesn't care. He knows what you need even if you don't. Hearing you say it is the only thing He needs. It's the sound of your own voice finally getting it. You are capable of so much more.

Six billion realizations radiate out from the planet every day like finger tips trying to stretch far enough to smudge the sky. Our souls struggle like drowning men as our bodies pull us back towards the earth. Sometimes we remember what we are meant to be: beautiful. I know because every face I've ever seen has my father's eyes.

But we forget what we're born knowing. We practice ugliness to hide ourselves from each other. We tell ourselves lies like loneliness, until we believe them. The preacher's got it wrong. Most people damn themselves.

But prayer is the simple truth of breathing into a receiver and knowing that someone on the other end can hear you. You don't even have to talk. Just take a deep breath and be yourself.

Amen.

Ayanna Boykins

Babes, Bitches, Divas…Lend me your ears

Allow me to clear matters that have plagued us for years,
Or brought tears from jeers, because we didn't fit the "mold".

Knee high to a grasshopper—we were brainwashed into becoming beauty queens
Lean…A sight to be revered—to be obtained.
But then we fell waste to file 13, shredded, because we weren't 10s
Plain face, pear-shaped, butt's too wide—pants that ride;
Big zits, small tits, lips too full, hair like wool…

Bad attitude, she's a prude
Caus' she won't put out, plus sized and rather stout...
Eyes too close, nose too large -
I don't like a woman who always takes charge.
Too smart, too dumb...
Is this enough to sum up the reasons why we have so many pairs of "issues"
in our closets, Ladies?

Babes, Bitches, Divas...Lend me your ears...

We've been reeled in hook, line and sinker
Fish nets full of regret
Causing manicured mental meltdowns,
With a matching "pedicured" psychosis.
Polished off with a top-coat of low self esteem...
All this to be deemed a queen?
I mean—Gaze into our eyes beyond the mascara, penetrating the colored
contacts
Viewing clearly—a doll of circumstance.
A mask to cover-up; blending blemishes to shield us from further exploitation.

Babes, Bitches, Divas...Lend me your ears...

Breast fed society's standards...
Suckling the silicon until we ooze—
Filled with the subliminal suggestions of day and night creams,
With dreams of a wrinkled-free façade.
But then our baby-phat yields to cellulite, and that ain't right!
So we nip and tuck and with a little luck,
Become beautiful in the eyes of...Man?
(Well, if dick size were measured in cup size, would all eyes prize his
lil' treasure?)

Babes, Bitches, Divas...Lend me your ears...

Have a little pride that you ride the crimson tide—
Don't be shy! Wear your thigh-highs and wade through the bullshit lies!
Don't be lipo-sucked or mind fucked into thinking that

Your $.75 to his dolla' don't "make me wanna holla…throw up both my hands."
Yea, you gotta "walk tall" and wear a padded bra if you must increase your bust.
Let your cup runneth over with notions of mental makeovers.
Augment your attitude to deal with self love,
Rather than rolling in the dough of Cosmos' cookie cutter concept
For you to immerge as a non-fat, whole-wheat, artificially flavored wafer.
Inject intellect rather than collagen…
Sinking the ships with loose lips as opposed to tight,
Preaching the "word" and our rights, from a non-skewed woman's point of view.

Babes, Bitches, Divas…Lend me your ears…

For I come to bring you peace of mind during times
When genital mutilation is still prevalent in countries,
And mastectomies still outnumber the removal of testes.
Voices may be silenced, faces and bodies may covered
Yet we have discovered that…
Frailty, thy name is NOT woman!

Sandra Brennan

Voted Nicest Girl

Under my senior picture in my yearbook is a caption
That reads "Voted Nicest Girl."
I gotta say that title has always pissed me off.
I wanted to be the sexy girl, the funky girl,
The too cool for school girl.
The most likely to go down on a married teacher,
Under the bleachers girl.
But no-I am, and will always be "the nice girl."
What few people know is that under this Marcia Brady-esque exterior
There is a seething sexy Catwoman dieing to come out and play.
I know that I could bring a man to his knees
With all I have inside me

And I've always thought that a man on his knees
…is a very, very good thing.
When they look at me, I know what they see…
A twenty-first century June Cleaver.
Someone who is good and kind,
Reliable and sickly sweet.
Someone who always remembers birthdays,
And cooks Thanksgiving dinner.
Someone who can be counted on
For 3 dozen cupcakes at each and every bake sale.
Someone who will never be late for carpool.
I am the one everyone writes in
As their emergency contact person
Because they know I will always be there…
Do you know how hard that is to live up to, some days?
I'm not saying that that isn't me, it is.
I admit it, grudgingly. I am "nice."
But there are days when this nice girl,
Gets tired of being so nice, so in control.
You look at me and see my smile and think, I'm wonderful, right?
I just got to say that sometimes…
Sometimes, appearances are deceiving.
Oh you don't want to know all the illicit thoughts
That travel through my head on a daily basis.
I think if someone opened my mind for the world to see
They would have me thrown in jail
And kept under lock and key.
Children would be told to stay away from me,
Old ladies would be scandalized and mortified
And men…men who want to take a walk on the wild side…
Who love to live dangerously…
Would be banging down my door.
You think nice girls only think nice thoughts?
Ha! A lot you know!
You have no idea of the erotic, exotic, triple X rated thoughts
That run through my mind, 24/7.
So sure, I'll feed your dog while your out of town
And baby-sit your kids, and make you soup when your sick,

But don't think, not for a moment, that that's all I am, or all I could be.
But you want to know what this nice girl wants most?
In a perfect world, I would find someone,
Who was voted Nicest Boy in his senior class,
Who thinks just like me.
Who is kind to strangers and animals, and loves kids
Who knows a thousand ways to please a woman
Using just his tongue…
Someone who will rock my world on Saturday night
And stand beside me in church, on Sunday morning.
I want a nice boy with a nasty, nasty mind who will love me just right.
Someone who will take out the garbage and fix my car.
Someone who knows how to make a woman scream and beg for more.
I'm looking for Ward Cleaver with a raging wild side.
I want someone who will love all the sides of me,
Who sees through the nice girl to the hot woman underneath
Someone who is solid but can satisfy.
Yeah, that's what this nice girl wants.

Mormons on Bicycles

I have a fetish for those boys
That travel in pairs.
Their crisply cut hair and
Stark white shirts,
The way their carefully knotted ties
Blow in the wind as they peddle furiously,
On their noble quest to save us all
From certain purgatory,
Or at least save all those who dare
To sit waiting at bus stops.
There is something about young men
with fresh scrubbed skin,
And a clean pure souls
That makes me want to whisper
My dirtiest thoughts in their ears,
And watch as faces turn red and hot,

And that look of innocence fade from eyes
As they realize that there are pleasures
To be had in this carnal Garden of Eden,
and I, the serpent tempting them.
I look at these young men in their prime
And can only think of my own tag-team fantasy
And want to send buttons flying as I rip
Open shirts and unbuckle and unzip as my lips
Travel down to the temple that I want to worship.
I want them to fill me with the holy spirit,
And make me scream out to God and Jesus,
And the heavens as I descend to that next plane
Of existence, where all is light and joy…
And heaven is mine…

Keith "Boogie" Brown,

Cell Phone Poem

Would you please leave that cell phone at home alone
Like that damn kid Macaulay Culkin

Cause no matter where I be there is always somebody
talking
Just over the horizon while on their Verizon
Wreckin while on their Erickson

And not quite realizing that they can't control a
Motor vehicle while on their Motorola

Causing me pain and migraines, swerving into my lane
Interrupting my morning serenity,
regardless of new laws that require a hands-free

and now my nerves is unraveling
cause whether I'm at movies, banks, restaurants, or

poetry gatherings,
there's always someone blabbering to the point where I
wanna throw blows and start jabbing

but not even Tyson or Roy Jones can withstand such
cell phone stamina
word warriors that never seem to get winded
as long as their night and weekend minutes are
unlimited

and maybe I probably wouldn't be complaining at all
if it wasn't for the fact that last night
I was interrupted by a booty call
During a booty call
And she answered it :>

Making me recall a time long before
This phone cell hell
When ma bell ruled everything around me and quarters
reigned supreme

And now I have a dream, like Martin Luther Jr. the
great
That one day
Everyone will reach down and put their cell phones on
vibrate

Not be judged by the color of their faceplate.

Not scream on their cell when their in the subway

Yes, I have a dream

that one day, I'll be able to go to the movies and
make it through a Jet Li flick

Without Tyrone and Laquita Ebert giving a cell phone
review of it.

Rapid cell phone charger, $24.99
Leather carrying case, $25.99
Hands Free Headset, $19.99

Leaving that cell phone home alone
PRICELESS

CAN U HEAR ME NOW?

Random Ramblin's

I call into question the sense and sensibilities of a president whose
Little Debbies are
about as wholesome as a pack of Twinkies
they conveniently come in two's
and their father's a Ding-Dong
So I throw American apple pie at white picket fences
And play batter up with mailboxes owned by the Jones'

Keep up with that
As I suffocate on carbon monoxide dreams of your SUV's
might as well be a PathFinder out in the Yukon because my

voice can't be heard above your Escalade escapades
But I can't quite climax because Hummers
don't feel as good when the price of oil has gone up to two soldiers a day

So I drive less and spend as much time walking in my Air Force Ones, as
Bush spends flying in his Air Force One,

And sometimes I feel no different cause I can smell the sweatshops on my
sweatsocks

But its all bizness
So I just do it,
because sometimes

even if you have the Answer.....
Your still destined to end up number 2
Ask Reebok for verification

Life is short, so play hard
Unless you live in nations where the U.S. Bogards
And then life is just short
Or life is just hard

Or life is just short and hard
And u can go kick rocks…

But not too far because you will probably need them again to throw strikes against the two tons of steel thats running over the tents in the refugee camps you called home

While in other time zones thousands cry as misplaced strikes allows two runs to reach home, they drink another beer, beat their wives, pet their dogs and then they go home
Stressed!!!
but
Stress is strapping a bomb on your sternum and knowing that you might still be alive when burning
But at least in death your voice is heard in spirit on CNN for ten seconds every twenty minutes for the rest of the day or until J LO decides to breaks up with Ben Affleck
And then fuck!!!
You just died in vain
Son of a bitch!!!

or son of a bush,
Either way its a push and I'm close to the ledge

And I might just SET IT OFF now there are almost as many banks as check cashing joints in my neighborhood.

And speaking of cashing checks, I'm not gonna Lynch Jessica for cashing in on a million dollar book deal, but why was Shoshana left holding her Johnson

Call this random ramblins or casual conversation

But a wise man once told me three things

He said "never turn your back on a proctologist"

There are no such things as wardrobe malfunctions

And

And "never trust anything that can be found on every street corner in the ghetto". So I say no to drugs, don't eat fried chicken, and I look at Chinese food veeeeery suspiciously.
One day I'll stop drinkin…
But for now I'm thinking, just how many chefs do you need to open up a chicken joint that sells seafood, tacos, pizza, and gyros,
The road to Cairo is paved with good intentions
But I have a feeling that Leroy's the only chef in the back
And he probably learned to cook in prison
He's mellowed out a lot
but send your food back at your own risk

and now i'm just rambling
because I'm pissed

And sometimes situations be enough to make me wanna slit my own wrist
But the good news is……………………

I saved 10% on my insurance by switching to Geico

JV Brummels

Downtown Slam

When Lisa Sandlin came north from Santa Fe to join the English Department at Wayne State College, she brought with her the idea for a slam. She'd attended one, or knew someone who'd attended one, or had read a newspapers article about one—I don't precisely recall—and that was enough to get us both excited. It seemed like something we ought to try.

For a while our slams were low-key, in-house affairs. In the fall semester, Lisa and I would each teach a beginning poetry workshop. During finals week, we'd take an evening, meet in the Humanities building lounge, and these two sections would face off. Usually, the members in the upper-level workshop would judge. We'd make quite a fuss over the competitive nature of the slam; for weeks before the slam students from opposing workshops would eye each other suspiciously in the halls. I would assure my students that they clearly had the advantage—I had read their poems and knew them to be excellent. Meanwhile, Lisa—from what our spies told us—would spend her workshops honing her students' delivery and, I suspect, doing some fashion makeovers. (I can't prove Lisa encouraged it as a way of gaining points from the male judges, but her female students tended to show up in hose and heels, or with bare midriffs; they also seemed to smile a lot and even occasionally wink.)

Only Lisa and I knew the competition was a sham. After a great show of gathering score sheets, tallying points and comparing notes, we would stand together and announce that "the winner is poetry!" That phrase was Lisa's idea, too. I'm not sure why we didn't play it as a straight competition. I suppose we had some notion that poetry shouldn't be competitive. I know several poets who still "don't believe in slams," despite their obvious popularity. Maybe it was just too much fun to say the truth, that poetry was the winner.

In most ways these "slams" weren't much different than the public readings many workshop teachers host for their students. I had done that for years. But a significant difference became obvious: the quality of the performances. Not only did these young poets slam with a kind of fire I had never heard in workshop readings, the performances gained dramatic power as the evening went on. Clearly, competition added an edge to the work, and, even more obviously, poets fed off each other, determined to outperform the poets who'd read before them. The result was an evening of poetry that built as it went on.

At this writing, SLAM XIII is about a month away. Wayne State hosts two slams a year, one each semester. My shaky calculations suggest, then, that the first downtown slam was in the spring of 1999, a fitting end to the old millennium and a nice kickoff to the new.

I suppose everyone involved was a little nervous about the first slam. Poets had read in bars before, of course, but these slammers would be mostly undergraduate English majors who tended to be more comfortable alone with a book than on a stage in front of an audience that was sure to contain at least a few drunks. The weather was cold and rainy. Lisa and I worked out a set of rules based on how we thought slams were run. (To this day, Wayne rules remain a little different from other slams.) Our secret weapon was Eddie Elfers, a seasoned performer, who had agreed to emcee the evening. (Eddie has hosted almost all of the subsequent slams; his good humor and ability to keep things moving along have contributed much to their success.)

That first slam was more successful than I could have imagined—packed house (including a good number of drunks), an awful lot of good poems and performances, close judging and a suspenseful finale. The downtown slams continue to be the highlights of the year for me.

Though lots of folks from out of town have competed and sometimes won, the core competitors continue to be Wayne State undergraduates. I've seen them hold their own against some very seasoned slammers, and that is an invaluable part of a literary education these days. What was, and continues to be, best in the slams are the surprises, when very young poets I've known only in a workshop appear to visibly grow in the spotlight, finding their voice to speak their piece to an attentive crowd. That moment, when an unprepossessing student morphs into a poet capable of dictating when the audience breathes, is magical.

And magic is what poetry is about. Magic can and does happen on the page, but the connection slams allow between poet and audience is both larger and more personal than the printed word. And it's reassuring, in a new century and millennium, to see that most ancient of the literary arts poetry return to its oral roots. When it comes to slams, Lisa has always been right: Poetry is the winner.

Erica Chu

We Need a Power Poem

We need a power poem
A wake up poem
An eat your breakfast, drink your milk
in the kitchen poem

A poem that
black babies, brown babies
yellow, red, and white babies
can grow up on
can eat, can drink, can live on
And never be weaned from

A power poem
A who you think you is poem
One with hands on hips,
eyebrows raised, and lips that know
you know she knows

When sisters stand tall
Elbows digging, smiles risen
Giggles scurrying around
In the back
the poem's rhythm keeps them standing strong

Sleepy-eyed, scared of life
Come running to her bed
Thunder crashing, lightning flashing
But we tremble alone instead

Where is the power poem?
That goads us, moves us,
leads us, is for us
the direction of our home?

It ain't here, so we wait
We live our lives and wait
We stand up straight
We clean our plates,
but hide under the covers and wait.

Nat Derickson

Lunch Card

On my first day of first grade the teacher
laid it all out for the class when she said,
"all of you who receive free lunch, free milk, free weekly reader,
bring your paperwork to my desk."

Not just once, but three times she said,
"all of you who receive free lunch, free milk, free weekly reader,
bring your paperwork to my desk."

As if poverty had left me deaf and stupid too,
I said sorta like poverty had left me deaf or stupid too,
I wish I would've know the words to say,
"SHUT THE HELL UP TEACHER I'M ON MY WAY,
and every kid in here heard you all three times!"

The walk, from my desk to her desk
through the runny nose, lost tooth, bowl cut
pencil sucking, booger eating gauntlet of strange looks
coming out of little eyeballs like
the little eyeballs had little mouths that we're saying,
"ha, ha, ha, Nat gets a free lunch, he can't afford it," this walk

was a forced march fueled by confusion,
because in my class of almost twenty-five
only three of us rose up to take our papers to the teacher.

Yes, I guess the teacher's lesson for the day was all about difference,
all about whose daddys were the haves and whose
daddys didn't have shit and I thought shit,
I never had to do this when I had me one them
things some called daddy—I paid for my morning dose of milk
in my Colorado kindergarten,
but now I was back in Nebraska and my daddy told me
when we left him just a few weeks before
we were only going back to grandma's for a visit,
while he held me like a starving junkie with
a sandwich in the left hand and a crack rock in the right
and he chose that crack, that woman living two building down
he chose that woman and sent us
all the way back to grandma's for "a visit."

For my first long day of first grade,
first day of being graded by the dollar sign,
first day of knowing I was one three fat "Fs"
in a class of twenty-five clueless, clean slates
scarred now by scratches from the first
pecks of the order that would sort us all someday,
someway someone would sort us into
some sort of sensible boxes,
boxes made to keep us in our places
face down against the grains of truth they think
were qualified enough to see if we can pay for lunch,
pay for a punch through a card for a steel tray
with a glob of god knows what steaming
by a piece of buttered white bread
green beans and tapioca pudding
all washed down by me with
puke warm FREE milk,
and just look at me now..............

Problem Child

Please allow me to scratch a scene across your mind
of a crushed kid stuck in a classroom corner
with a knotted, empty belly and a frightened mind,
he's got a tag upon his head says he's a problem child.

But—the problem is the problem child's mama's
working nine to five talking and typing and jumping
everytime the big boss barks for more, then
six to twelve—ringing up gas and big gulps
cringing everytime the harsh words come
across the counter from the townsfolk,
cutting her down or stripping her bare
with lewd stares paired with whistles or
"hey baby whacha doing later,"
she replies to all with cold eyes and sharp thanks
sounding a little bit like,
"your done here now so get the hell away from me."
So the townsfolk taking their things and go,
some mumbling as they're leaving,
"Jesus, what the hell is her problem?"

Well, her problem is her problem child's daddy
feels dead without a job so he spends
his nights in a chair with a dozen beers and a ballgame
while the problem child rots in his room
wasting bad guys with lasers and AK-47s
on the fifty-fourth level of the latest play station creation
'til the top lids of his wired eyes droop
to meet the bottom and his head snaps back
against his bed's edge and he falls asleep
sitting up on the floor with a joystick
stuck in his hand and the t.v. screen flashing,
"game over," over and over and over.

Hush little problem child sleep in peace,
you must drop this day and dream,

this long day of being laughed at and left out
on the playgrounds edge, at the one empty
table in a packed gym choking down a free lunch
flipping through a comic book acting like
your solitude is fine in your classroom corner
where you're feeling like an island
in a vibrant sea of life where you
cannot find a way to swim
so you sink a little deeper everyday,
hush little problem child sleep in peace,
because the same damn day is coming soon.

Meanwhile an info-mercial glows
through his home's living room,
feeding get rich schemes into
his drunk daddy's head,
his daddy's head is sunk low now,
got his chin dug into his chest,
drool is oozing out amidst
short tortured breaths keeping beat
between long deep snores until the back
door creaks and the problem child's mama
sneaks in like an angel and she puts her boys to bed.

She works the big one first,
with a soft kiss on a long whiskered cheek and a tight
squeeze of her drunk man's one beer can-less hand
then she leads him down the hallway past the bathroom
on the left and the problem child's lair on the right
to the end at the center where their bed rests.

Then she doubles back to the problem child's lair
where she finds her little man like he gives up every night,
but the notes on the floor
amidst the empty pop cans and chip bags
are for level fifty-four of the latest play station creation,
and she recalls last night's scribbles were for
level fifty-three, so all she sees is progress,

she can't see the t.v. screen flashing "game over,"
all she sees is the baby she gave birth too
as she pries him from his shag carpet saddle
she sees no problem, she only sees the same
damn day coming way too soon.

When

When this war is over,
the world will live in peace.

A terrifying peace possible only
just past a massive flash of violence making
everybody take a sad step back and say,
"oh my god, what the hell have we begun."

We will be shocked,
slack-jawed and awed by the way we
set the whole world aflame
one cruise missile at a time like a
thousand matches flicked on a dry straw pile
ringed by burning oil-soaked sand and
smoldering heaps of humanity locked in unity against us
when this war is over.

When this war is over,
the Bush Boys better have the goods,
I want to see VX and anthrax and germs of all sorts,
I want to see blueprints and plans photos of
American land and crystal clear dots connected by
deep lines in the sand leading all the way back to Baghdad.

When this war is over,
I'm going to watch the Iraqi people gag as
they take their first force feeding of the
Bush Boy's recipe for happiness
right-wing American style.

We're going to make them just like us,
frightened divided and vicious.

We're going to make them think like us
"like I've got to earn I've got to spend I've got to own
got to like got to cheat got to steal got to feel this world
is here for nothing and no one but you."

We're going make them feel like us,
over-worked, underpaid and frantic,
spiritually shattered from our scatter-brained train of thought
that keeps the lie alive that the few can have a lot
and those who have not got must learn to swim or
we will let them sink see this is how our leaders think
you beautiful liberated Iraqi people and
this is how they're going to lead you too you've
become our nation's fifty-first state and just look
at our list of locations and fates
for states 52, 53 and 54
my god may Allah bless and protect
us all through this terror war.

Katie F-S

13: Two Bits

I got a haircut.
I got them all cut.
I cut it all off, my absent big-cat mane,
my main missing link to my femininity,
and I think my mother is pissed.
I am shorn like a ewe, and you
cannot imagine how I haven't missed
my lioness's tresses.

Her dead-end objection, devoid of inflection, insists:
"You had such pretty hair, you had
sunset hair, you had tangled-knotty-curly
hair that obscured an auburn sky."
But Ma, now it's funky hair,
now it's easy hair, now I can wash my hair
six times an night and it will dry exactly right
every sudsy time.
Now it's a radical liberal political rhyme.
Now it's scalp-rooted poetry: the less that's there,
the more significant my statement.
Now it reflects the unrestrainable, irreplaceable,
personable, personal
ME.

She lectures like a sonorous sewing machine:
"You look like a boy."
Mom, you mean I look like a dyke.
I knocked you off-kilter and the ponytailed filter
that allowed your perspective of
nearly-straight Kate
has been clipped. The closet is clear-cut.
My slate is full up with this silent scrawlin'—I
will not let you pretend to ignore the
forest that's fallen from my face.
I am stark, I am satiated in this suddenly-sparse
space, I am uncomplicated without
cornrows of cautious trees. I am caged neither by
the scabs of a boy nor
the arms of a man.
I am free.
Besides, Big Mama, dig my breasts,
dig my hips,
dig this sarcastic, cynical, shit-eating grin
pussyfooting across my lips—
dig this salty sugarshockin' stanza,
then hold my green dragon eye and tell me,
ain't I a woman, Mother whip-strong and smart,

ain't I?

Her dialtone diatribe plods on:
"You'll be alone for the rest of your life."
Mother.
O Mother.
Last night I discovered the shape of my head.
Last night I shed my last unearned vanity—
what a travesty, that barretted keratin is
beheld as beauty, but my fuzzy silhouette is
insufferably unlovable. Should I
shave and snip and twist and grow
into this newest feminist
Emancipated Liberated Womanhood Mold?
Should I hold my chin against my chest in
bald, bold penance?
I have taken the path less split, less ending,
I have taken to befriending
each brief breeze that breaks
across my crown.
I will not take this shit lying down.
I will not regard independence as an impediment.
Ain't no one can prevent this
witchy warrior invocation:
Today I stave off cellular, soul-ular starvation.

She lets go of her breath like a derelict daughter:
"I just want someone to love you."
Ah. But I savor that which I lack—
for hair, like a parent's favor,
usually grows back.

September 2003: The Emergency Room

Had it been me, with the rain bouncing
ground-ward like swear words or gravel
at the unraveled end of another almost-

dead day—had it been me, trapped
by the blacktop of beasts and machines and
earth-bound by the burden of dreams
too complex to convey, but someday,
yes someday yes we will someday—
had it been me, Matt, had they asked me
whether I am gay, I would have swung
away and let my receding steps replace the poetry.
I would have let the slant of my shoulders say
everything—I would have let my lips lay
down and sleep. Midnight and me fail to astound
would-be parking-lot prophets, so that these
men spray profanity against our profundity
and slay us famous via television and various
mediated derision—yeah, we fail. And so
I give back their midnight. I return to them
their danger. I refuse their demands to derange
my own rate of exchange as if I were
faceless at war and would wager
my lover's eardrum, perforated, against
everyone else's vindicated safety.
I relinquish the delusion that any blood-
born freedom is a victory: in the aftermath
of any back-alley brawl, who's left satisfied,
and who's left the backlash?
Had it been me, I would have packed
my pride hip-deep and critical and shot
not even eye contact toward the political
chimera prowling our dark legislative
dead ends. I have more appalling stuff
to offer than bared fangs or bruises;
battles rage that we must fight and
fights that we can choose. Let me lose this
revolution that renders scarce safety so
much less elusive that we pursue scarecrow
execution, like our gunny-sack heads were
straw-stuffed and hung, like we were any of us
young enough to be offering up pieces or high-

strung crucifixions. Matthew—o, Matthew.
I am not brave. I have no heart.
This hollowed world with its perils grave-
deep and real and its furious moonstone reeks
some midnights of Laramie. Had it been me,
I would have followed
the high yellow road
home.

A VALENTINE WITH WINGS
(o icarus o)

Today, a bird
          dropped—no,
bullet
drilled
down
from the blue and hazy sky.
I dreamed,"Suicide
or poison—neither here
nor there when the air
                (disappears)
inside and below. In the end, when
death says, rain, we go."
Still I seem to be a storm
that hasn't struck sidewalk
                or stone
even here, where the bones
of this planet poke past her skin—
and she is resplendent in all
her stark-sunset glory, but
even best friends' smiles stretch
thin here like our teeth
are where hurt forced
its way
     through
          so our words

sound like wounds, and the land
lays so bare here, and the trees
crook like angels paralyzed
in prayer—small
wonder:
we would rather split open
our ribs to the empty
atmosphere
than pack our hearts
with corn fields—or wheat—
and push back upright.

It's love, I think, and its
incarnation in this zeitgeist,
promising us backbreak
and drought.
                    Have you seen
the ripped and melancholy
nothing that blankets
alfalfa in the spring? If it's
love
you think you need,
have mine. I will love you with
daisies and picnics and tickets to
Leonard Cohen somewhere smoky
and red as a pigeon's
thrumming undercarriage.
I will love you with haiku:
You want a puppy
to name Bruce. I can afford
this coloring book.
I will love you with my
breath and my hands: this
                    space
beside me while I sleep
can happen in the exact shape of you
wrapped up pretty-please
in a two-thirty telephone call

if you're losing
by degrees
the distinction between flight
and freefall.
        I will love you
revolutionary-style, cognizant
of our flaws, but confident of
our capability.
        I am weary of playing
Impenetrable, as if art were
another word for armor—I.
        Am.
        Not.
Machinery. I am but
a crabgrass blade, and I
will paint green this whole
fucking globe from under
their feet if they don't care to look
down
and recognize who stands
guard between them and the void—
and how vastly we outnumber them.
We have won
an unquestioning victory: we are
here; we know how to survive.
I love you.
Now: thrive.

Brian Finn

Love and Lucifer's Mallards

So my buddy chad, he sez, write a poem about satan
and I sez, satan, man, satan.
Satan is a fickle thing, a fickle fickle thing, see.
Some say he exists,

some say he's here,
some say he's a fickle thing.
Fickle fickle thing—quick now DUCK—

SUCK A DUCK
mallards and Donald and Daffy and Aflac
and Darkwing and Daisy and Tales, Duck Tales—WOO-OO!
My guess is that *if* satan is real
he would SUCK LOTS OF DUCKS
and his favorites would be mallards.

That's absurd, man, but satan, man,
he doesn't exist
but you see you ask one roman collar and you ask another
and they all both won't every one of them *all* tell you
that satan is a real physical manifestation of evil
who lives in fiery pits and brandishes a pitchfork
and he can kiss my hairy white ass with his horns
cuz he thinks he's all red and he's gotta tail and El Diablito,
gotta Hail Satan, I'm the god son of the school of thought that sez THIS

and listen well: there is no hell, but maybe there is
and there is no heaven but *if* there is
there *was* a guy in red pajamas
who put up a fight cuz he was the most beautiful angel
and was jealous of you and me
and if you ask, I'll tell, and think you'll agree
that Hollywood has it all wrong
cuz the most beautiful angel definitely didn't look like
Oh God, George Burns, big cigars, You Devil
or even Al Pacino in that film where that guy who plays Neo
was the advocate to the devil—man what does he know?

I'm advocating not knowing but assuming
and making an ass out of mainly just me
you
see
that

satan *is* not, but *does* grow
in the hearts of children, yes, children
who tear limbs off insects and tell lies
who then grow up to demoralize
the aspirations and dreams of those wretched nonbelievers

these children then rollers with their bake sale pies
in the name of all holy to fund hate rallies
against gays and women-who-just-want-a-choice
man we gotta voice our opinion
and say brothers and sisters keep on livin'
and do what you gotta do
and *what you gotta do* is not buckle
under no deity-of-questionable-existence's *followers*
who misconstrue and piss on His word
it was LOVE.

Followers of that same Him are confused and ignorant
-or-
belligerent and with bad intent
and do wicked things in His name;
things like oppress, generally screw things up
and make a big ole mess
and I say Satan is in *their* hearts
even if he is no physical manifestation

but just the idea itself
it's alive alive alive in their hearts
and it tears mine apart
to think that we not only have to perpetuate it's existence
but then manifest it and give it a name
and it's name is Satan or Lucifer or Legion or Scratch...

let not that E-word hatch
an egg to be a VILLage
of degenerate thought in your brain
and then bring all to shame
with bass-ackwards actions and organized factions

against all things good

and you see good is not necessarily holy
because holy is a sometimes dirty word
in the eyes of ones who need not a book
or an organization that just wants fear-cash
to tell you to LOVE

as that one big good guy says
but I'm not sure
if
ever
he
was
ever
around
either

I'll tell you if He *is* that no *good* physical manifestation
would make up a thing like damnation
just love man
love love love thy neighbor

that's all you need to know
not who begat whom
and who had a big friggin boat when the storms raged
under some commanding egotistical wrath
and if you ask me the alpha and the omega are one
and that one is satan
cuz satan's commanding and egotistical and evil, right?

and he doesn't know the meaning of love
or maybe he does and just never got hugs
you know it bugs me to know no way
out of this metaphysical mess
of who is real and who is not real
and maybe you aren't and maybe I aren't
and I say *darn't!*

satan still *might* but probably *might not* be real
and if he is, HE'D SUCK MALLARDS
because that's just as absurd
anyway you look at it below or above
as that one word that's misconstrued into hate:
LOVE, man, LOVE—
Sorry, Chad, but your Satan poem turned into a poem about Love

Notes From a High School Class

—To Sarah B.

i
sit here listening with one ear
and comprehending with no brain as my two eyes
wander
to the corners of the
universe
yet still feeling my uncomfortable school desk chair.
i smell the hair of the
girl
in front of me and i am odorifically delighted
with a lightly perfumed breeze.
i taste the walls of this
righteous
cavern, it's stalagmites and stalactites loosely
gnawing
on a rubbery sticky blob of sugary fresh breath
which was certainly not promoting tooth
decay.
vibrations of
language
emanating from a deep dark mineshaft
sound shaky and confused with its opinionated
exclamations.
i sigh and sink heavily into my seat, my eyelids

heavier yet dropping the curtain over
reality
replacing it with an opaque
oblivion
of black and red
tumbling and playing off each other
in a rhythmic dance of
aimless
chaos avoiding the
real world
as i am beaten down
the life wrestled out of this haggard
soul
agitated and festering from battles with itself.
lost.
where do i go now?
i mean what happens when the physical plane
is spent once more
and i tangent off into the infinite fifth
dimension
tumbling and tossing confused and
lonely
yet not really caring? i'll land and stop being lost
but found laughing, relieved
at what a rollercoaster it's been.
but that may never happen.
what's over the next hill on this twisting dangerous
torturous path of suffering, hallucinogens, and pain?
"it's going to get better," she
screamed
into the night
possibly not believing it herself
just as lost and confused as I
but with hope on her side
on this endless rainbow
with its mythical pot of gold.
the treasure better get here fast
as i am nervously

shaking
my arm pumping ejaculations of ink and
thought
onto a thin sheet of
raped
forest and listening with
one
ear to the voice of
reason, morality, authority, and bullshit.
amen.

Charles Fort

The Blues Guitar

One can learn about the blues living in White Clay during a killer frost and by picking from the stem of winter collards, and the phantom notes of the blues can be taught by listening to the chorus under the bare feet at dawn under the pine and snow, by the meeting of stone and water, and the splitting seed. The windows are breaking in the storm cellar. There is a clock radio with large brown dials on the screen porch. The blanched hooves of the farm animals thunder in their floating stall. One can sing about digging up mud and potatoes for two world wars and countless half-world wars. How does one keep time to music planted with a hoe and groomed by a tiller which turns out a tune accompanied by a single inhuman voice and then thrives like a congregation walking into the baptismal waters? One uneven step into the winter garden and nothing in the soil can be saved. The moaning chords of the blues echo behind each ball and chain and one hides where one can sleep.

[previously published: *Darvil*, 1993. St. Andrews Press]

Dog Tag Rag

This journey from Asia to the Middle East to Central America begins at 3:00 a.m. inside a concrete shelter beneath a ghetto in Detroit and we lift our parachutes and sit still and wait for the red light. We leave the Concorde and land on our feet near a battery of beardless classmates and blue collar workers in a private duel for pension and prayer. The lottery of ball and chain at 6:00 a.m. We kneel for hours. We drag our ankles and toes and lift our buttocks to sixteen needles. Plasma drains from our noses. The arms grow long and wary. We are the invisible men looking for a one year fix, human vampires who bomb the soft church bell and hospital bed. High Noon. Darvil listens to the Motown sound and a rotating world grates under his feet. He shines his black boot with liquid morphine. He carries one blind eye of the enemy in a glass jar. He writes a post-card to his grandmother. It bears his signature and serial number. She receives the glass jar and a miniature flag. She dances a dog tag rag and collapses at the kitchen door. The young soldier's helmet is tossed into a body bag stuffed with congressional stars. Your life and your name are written in a book. This is your life son.

[previously published: *Darvil*, 1993. St. Andrews Press]

Darvil Meets James Brown in Harlem and New Orleans

Please, Please, Don't Go
Harlem. 1962. Apollo Theater. Ain't no potato like blackberry jam. Darvil sits three rows and three hours before show time front stage his elephant ears and alligator eyes drift to a black cajun a drummer like a waterfall in the rocky mountain fat back Americana rent party on a twenty four hour street corner rock and roll born and stamped grade A by the bastard blues and subway humming birds feed on race records found sunny side up on a brownstone Victrola 78's thrown to a black bottom mama by a big daddy in a nine piece suit woven in the harlem renaissance fire hydrant hot sauce hand out by a social worker in a farmer's market mango pie in the glove compartment of a three story Cadillac collards in every black ass pot a green banana in every two door garage mast head alley cat wrecking crew in grand central station grease on the ankle shoe shine pullman porter on a bag pipe anchors away on a continent of the five and dime window cleaner on the fifty-nineth floor juke joint catfish band in New Orleans. Try Me. 1982. Mississippi Queen floats on a red river midnight saxophone like a full moon carousel of bourbon and beer baroque barbecue goat ribs alligator pie mardi gras mambo street car lizard smokes a cuban cigar five minutes to show time ain't no potatoe like blackberry jam.

[previously published: *Darvil*, 1993. St. Andrews Press]

Monica Fuglei

Slam

In his white-walled office we sink into whiter chairs
to discuss last week's slam—
HE didn't do well,
and he says he doesn't like slam,
says he thinks it's all shock and leftist anger,
all he hears is *whose pussy, my pain*, or *masturbation*,
says this is no language of Keats,
you must be minority or extreme left to compete,
says it's all political,
all shock and violence,
it's all, each and every bit of it,
not
poetry.

He teaches poetry
and he knows poetry,
and I know that he knows poetry
like others know art in museums
or animals in zoos,
his poetry is kept in classrooms,
reigned in with words like scansion, signmatism, and syntax,
stuck in stanzas of black space on white pages,
and like a caged lion it paces,
and paces,
and paces,
searching out cracks or spaces between bars
to explode and escape.

And sometimes it shocks,
and sometimes it's violent,

and sometimes it's political,

and he's never seen that animal,
never known the beauty of she-clac she clac shackles
because he couldn't find it in the dictionary.
He says poetry has rules we most follow.

He can't see that slam
is that animal escaped,
the lion dancing down the streets,
taking over pages and stages,
it is the art woven into our day to day lives,
the dancing and loving and music and rhyming
that we live out our time in,

and yes,
some of us are left wing,
some are right,
some winged and wingless,
some have pussies and others dicks,
some spend our days jobless or childless
while others live their lives in collars of blue or white,
some are criminals and some are not,
some are black, white, red, yellow and everything in between,
some are political and some are not.

What then
do we have in common?
What we have in common is
this is about us
and we,
oh we,
we love words;
what they do and how they do it.
We don't splay out our poems on pages,
tack them down with pins
and gut them for all to see.

We catch those poems, those words,
we love them, caress the edges of words others avoid,
touch spaces and places that they will never go,
we map out the universe to pass to our children,
we swaddle and coddle phrases,
wrap our energy around phonemes,
and cry out when the rhyme's not quite right,
or when we need words to fight injustice.

So yes, Slam is not poetry,
slam is poetry plus.
Slam is us,
it is about us,
about who we are,
and we are—we are
word warriors, word lovers, word creators,
we are Slam.
We are.

Dominique Garay

Heat

My hand is tan
all the way through winter
my blood is warm
and that includes my heart

the winds are cold
and so are people
but I will remain warm

and I will warm others
like my grandmother's covers
the ones in patches

I Used To Be Brown

I used to be brown
but I've turned kinda white
and it's taken some time
it didn't happen overnight

I used to just speak Spanish
until I started watchin TV
then Deputy Dog and Sesame Street
got a hold of me

I grew up on a farm
people came there to eat
pickin asparagus, tomatoes and corn
no neighbors across the street

Imagine this kids reaction
when I discovered Dairy Queen
McDonalds and Coke
and that crown they gave you at Burger King

I started goin to school
but few where like me
my lunch in a sack
tortillas with beans

I'd jump off the bus
runnin down the hill kickin up dust
the kids would be screamin "go Speedy Gonzalez go!"
But that wasn't my last name
it was Sanchez
but to them just the same

I used to be brown
but I've turned kinda white
and it's taken some time
it didn't happen overnight

I started dating girls
these strawberry blonds
brunettes with milky white skin
and they inspired my songs

And though the allure
of chocolate is strong
when I crave vanilla
I see nothing wrong

And I heard "you're Chicano, Cubano, Latino, Hispano
leave them wedas alone!
Que no vez—can't you see they're not like you or me
stick to your own!"

I'm not putting up walls
I'm tearnin em down
there's too much beauty out there
that's left to be found

I used to be brown
but I've turned kinda white
like café con leche
I think it's all right

Because it's not about color
It's not about race
the way someone talks
or features on their face

It's always been about people
and making real friends
It's about being a spirit
and that never ends

I might drop this body
right here on the ground

disappear like a whisper
less than a sound

And when I come back
who knows what color I'll be
but one thing is for sure
I will always be me

Bodhi

Millions of years in a sea of oblivion
took me thousands of lives just to see what I've been livin in
a life of lies, confusion and doubt
I lived in fear and knew nothing about
the truth of the matter, the life of love
I had no idea what I was thinking of
I had dreams and desires and threw them away
I was haunted by my past and it stood in my way
but my life today has been changed
its been organized and rearranged
I'm headin forward towards my goal
of total freedom, a liberated soul
equal justice for all and freedom of speech
freedom of religion, this is what we should teach
to be your own advisor and make your own decisions
don't let other peoples lies blur your visions
because it's all about awareness, ethics and trust
being true to your own goals is definitely a must

See nothin' can touch me tonight
I am light, I'm the blue midnight
my eyes glow bright and I'm just outta sight
it's all tight as in the parts fit in just right
I guess I'm winnin the fight but no struggle
there's no counter intention no trouble
clean and clear with no fear like a bubble
just floatin around, barley touchin the ground

and the sound of stars from far away
singing to me, they got somthin to say
you gotta play
there's no fee tonight, I don't pay
things are just sorta goin my way
the essence of me I convey
with rhyme, on time no fallin off the line
it's all mine
some wanna make it a crime
but my shine, like sparkling wine
like fingers lightly dancing up and down your spine
take the time
to let love roll off of your tongue
to have fun, to be young and to just be
like you're free
like you're on ice in the sky
softly, gently,
breathing cool life
breathing cool life

Randy Gustafson

Envy In The Smoke

Still bathed in the sticky, sick film of cigarette
smoke exhaled from other people's lungs…I write.

What the hell am I doing up here?

What is it really like to cast off on a
stream of conscious so moving, so deep, so thick
with ideas that each time you dip your paddle in
another unconscious metaphor floats to the suface,
waiting to be gutted and multiplied, fed to the
hungry 5,000 like some consecrated manna of truth?

What manner of manifested
genius can take a pinch of philosophy,
a dash of psychology, a heaping scoop of comedy
and turn tragedy into a tasty masala that
always fills you up, yet leaves you craving more?

Apparently these gifts offered to amuse the muse can,
in lesser hands, abuse the muse who offers
trinkets of meter and beads of thyme that will never
be enough to buy back what was never yours to begin with.

I witness these flights of fancy take wing,
soaring so close to the sun I want to scream,
"Look out! You'll burn!! You'll catch fire!!!"
then they do and then they fall,
like ash from the cigarette, that produced
the smoke, that covers me once again
in spoken word envy.

Cath Haftings

Walt Whitman At A Slam

Singing about himself
wondering
will anyone get it?

Wild man image
might help
and there's a cute
boy in the front row.

He sings to that boy
as clearly and quietly
as he can

while hoping that the
words can be heard
still make sense
off the page.

Sweating when finished
but the applause appears
real, loud.

Until time penalty announced,
scores weren't bad.

Maybe next time,
He'll cut a bit.
Maybe.

Hard to sing of self
in three minutes.

Elliot Harmon

Luke

You're so lost and confused until some
quiet but funny person awakens you
to the mysterious joy of life, right?
It's that story. The one where
you're feeling so overburdened
with the bills on your table
and the white in your collar
and along comes someone.
Oh, and there's the moment when
you see them out picking daisies or
reading poetry to the squirrels at the park or
playing dulcimer on the curb of a dirty gas station,
and then later you go out

rolling down hills, or
catching frogs, or
dancing in the hail, and
suddenly you feel like a kid again and the world feels like a
    spontaneous place again where you're really free to be
    whoever you want.

"Your name's Luke," she says.
"How did you know that?" Luke says.
"I don't know," she says. "I just knew.
You want to see where I go look at stars?"
It turns out to be the top of an abandoned club downtown.
"Where did you get the keys to this place?" Luke asks.
Jennifer shrugs. It's so beautiful.
And there, before all the stars and the noisy Main Street,
Luke tells her how much he hates his job and his bosses
and himself. She mainly smiles.
They talk, or rather he talks, late into the night,
and eventually they doze off together on the top of the building.
He'll remember this as the night he felt
like he could become anything.

So here's a spontaneous idea.
What if you wake up the next morning with the quiet, funny person
and you leave? You see her at the theatre
a few days later and ignore her
or what if you catch cold from all that running around in the rain
    and fall dead,

your last words being something about that work assignment you
    wish you'd gotten to.
Do you really think
no one dies with
work on their minds?
I sure don't.

What if you wake up before she does
and oh so gently nudge her

off the building? How's that
for spontaneity?

What if there is no
mysterious joy of life? What then?
What if it's just us and whatever we make of it and what if
I want to live my quiet self without the daisies and the squirrels
    and the dulcimers?
What then?

Because what you can't see when you're there on the phone
is that the people in the other cubicles
are as incurable
as you.
And when people say society no longer needs God
they are really saying, "There is no way everyone
can be this lonely."
And the most repulsive supervisor you've ever had
also cried on the way out of the parking lot.

And what if that quiet, funny girl goes to a therapist
every day to help her understand
why she builds all these walls
of mystery over her guilt and self-hatred and
what if every time she makes that funny half-laughing smile
it's not because of some secret joke but to conceal
that she's jealous of you?
What then?

What if we'd rather fuck up sometimes
and come home to our roommates
who fuck up sometimes and admit,
on days when they're sick of finals and each other, that
there is really no joy to be found?

Because it's them—your joyless,
ugly, flawed, imperfect friends—
who'll be there when you wake up and eat Cocoa Pebbles with you

silently not trying to convince you it'll get any brighter.

Luke, don't settle.
You can do without Jennifer and her freaked out joy of life.

What if you answer the phone every day for thirty years
to people who hate you
and you never leave the the sterile white halls before dark
and you drive home exhausted
knowing there will be nothing there
but your loneliness and your friends
and what if you love it?

[previously published: *Luke, Don't Settle!*, 2004. Morpo Press]

Cricket to Grace

You ever notice at the open mics that the only people who cry
    onstage
are there to get credit for a class? Is that sad?

You still studying for that
Russian Realism test, by the way?
Let's get together and read The Cherry Orchard. You be
all the women, I'll be
all the men.

Won't it be gorgeous? We'll spend the night
talking around the subject and averting
the issue and almost
kissing
and when you fail the test
it'll be such a minor detail
that you might not even notice.

Chekhov was a doctor. That's way too much
grad school for a civilized man,

but it made him understand which things
really make a scene happen. In the end,
it's not about saving the orchard. All scenes
have only one arc:
two people almost share themselves
but get distracted by the luggage.

"Why is Liubov kissing the bookcase?" the
directors and scholars ask. "What does
she really want?" Do you want to tell them
there's no answer, or should I?

That whole conflict between Stanislavski and Chekhov—
overplayed. And ever since then there have been these
poor actors in studios everywhere in the world
trying to think their hardest
about their mothers and their childhoods
and that embarrassing sexual incident
from when they were eighteen,
when really they should be trying their hardest
not to think about those things.
Stanislavski read the scripts right; that's not
the problem. He just didn't get
how sexy futility can be.

And I have to think, if you'll pardon the tangent,
that it's the same problem
suffered by only the really good writers.
The ones who piece together their most hidden thoughts,
whose every poem could bring the audience to laughter
or tears as though they lived in some bizarro world
in which the people really want to laugh or cry or yearn.
Me, I prefer this world.

How many perfect poems have been aborted
when their scriptors said, "No, I don't think this'll
cause any convulsions."
And how many actors, at their peak, have said,

"I can't play that part yet; I don't have the depth."
These things sometimes happen to normal guys too,
not just the ones with depth.

When did we start believing
that unless we're living some impassioned lives
of tears and screams and laughter,
we're not real artists? We're not real lovers?
And forever banished is the thought that maybe it's a lie.
And just maybe we should tell our drama coaches,
our creative writing teachers,
our slam judges,
to shove it.
Maybe we should just stand up and say the words and maybe
the audience will be grateful.

One more question.
How many handsome young men will leave your doorstep,
you dryly confessing that you just don't feel anything for them,
and returning to your cold, white chamber to wait
for love to descend?

[previously published: *Luke, Don't Settle!*, 2004. Morpo Press]

Poem

Isn't it odd to notice that everyone
you call "friend" has been your friend
since you were ten years old?
And the people who,
in some sense, know you—what kind of drunk
you are, what you kiss like, what kind of poet
you wish you were—get relegated
to a part of your mind far away
from the place where you keep the moments you spent
on playgrounds with what
you now call your friends.

Collaborator. Drinking buddy. Roommate. They're all
shorthand for "person I never played
Foursquare with."

On a side note, I've not been sleeping lately.
I write for an hour or two, fall asleep at three,
and wake up at five, awake. And
that's what's gotten me thinking—

Well, here.
There was these berries on a tree
in front of my house when I was a kid.
I wish I knew what kind, but I don't. They
was really tiny and my Mom always told me
they was poisonous. So I shouldn't eat them.
That's like my first memory—"don't eat those."
Sometimes I look forward to you leaving
for a weekend or Christmas. Because that's
when we'll kiss goodbye
and share a pot of coffee without
talking about someone's latest project.
But I remember going entire weeks of my childhood
waking up before sunrise thinking about the berries.
Not enticed, necessarily—just overwhelmed.

I stood guard, sort of, when there were other kids
over. I took it upon myself to warn the world.
"Don't touch those!" I said in that loud voice
children use to send each other announcements.
"They're poisonous!"
You don't ask me much, and I guess
I'm grateful. You don't know the things
about me that only people's friends are allowed
to mention.
Stories that everyone pretends are made less
distressing by the silvery film that collects
on them over time but really aren't.
And you smile at me as you tell my friends

on the phone that I'm not here,
never asking why.

You sneak up behind me and place your
cold hand on my neck. "What'cha writin'?"
I tell you I'm doing a piece about friendship.
You sarcastically gasp, worried I've lost my edge.

How could I not have? Of course I ate them.
Fifteen or sixteen, telling myself it was an accident.
Their bitter taste lasted days,
and after that I had to wait for the awe to come back,
which it did in a month, before I could try again.
And that's what I was thinking about
when I woke up at five today.
I came downstairs and you were asleep on the couch
warmly bundled in your new boyfriend's arms.
Did you hear me come down? I don't know,
but you opened your eyes just then and
gave me that funny eyebrow thing. I smiled back
and you were asleep.
The berries are not a device.

[previously published: *Luke, Don't Settle!*, 2004. Morpo Press]

Heidi Hermanson

1,001 loads of laundry

Oh sure. It couldn't be 1001 pieces of Godiva chocolate
or 1001 dollars…OK.

Give me clean
    laundry
Wicker baskets, colorful bouquets
    in bloom

Cheerful scents wafting across the room.

1001 wrinkled old women
lovingly pinning it piece by piece on a line
A line of dancers
floating languidly in the breeze
Cumulous clouds in bright blue sky.

Some days I feel rumpled
A crumpled pile of laundry
Dreaming I'm drowning in a sea of clothes
I flail among sheets and pillowcases,
agitating briefs and t-shirts,
I spin-cycle through my day
while dreaming of oversize fluffy white towels
Soft as June air
To press my face in.

I pay as I go,
Hand-washing my ideas one at a time

The litany of the laundry:
Dark————————————————white
Dark————————————————white

Let's call for the integration of all laundry
1001 colors mixing together
1001 socks reunited at last
Let us all be the Ghandi of laundry, non-
violently resisting stains and wrinkles.

Let there be peace
and let it begin
in my washing machine.

And remember:
After enlightenment,
The laundry.

Con Agra Catacombs (The Chris Murray Poem)

—after A Supermarket in California

Dear Chris,
As I meander through
underground links
in search of an art fix,
my mind runs wild.

Oddly lit subterranean corridors
that snake around the corporate campus
seem more fit
for psychiatric rehabilitation
or secret society induction.

The perkiest elevator music, piped in
plays incessantly
only adds to the surreal quality…

Probably has subliminal messages
embedded therein:
Buy Healthy Choice

The tunnel dead-ends
and the mighty PR machine appears:
A wall-sized commerical that
would give Times Square pause.

Speaking of target audiences
Or maybe captive audiences?

"We produced 80,000 miles of Slim Jims
this year, enough to wrap around the world
3 and a 1/2 times."

Yes, they do everything from saving the earth
to feeding hungry children.
A benevolent Big Brother, if you will.

Currier and Ives prints
adorn the walls of the tunnels
But listen:

There be albinos, General Tom Thumb
and the famous Chang and Eng twins
sandwiched between Cutty ships,
pastoral scenes
and kittens eyeing goldfish in bowls.

Chris, you're the last person I need to tell
There's a freak show in eveyone.

Fingering my beads,
I shot out of my body:
Our lady of perpetual hallucinations
help me

I sincerely hope your sense of direction
is better than mine
I may never find my way out.

Jack Hubbell

Under Nat's Thumb (for Nat Derickson)

Nat says I have to open up and express myself.
He says I have to peel away all those layers of machismo
and reveal my effeminate inner core.
Nat says I should write poetry.
All I have to say is, "bullshit."

Nat says I should stop drinking beer [yea…right.]
and start hanging out in coffee shops.
He says I should start reading Sydney Sheldon
and Jackie Collins.
Nat says I should give him all my Bukowski
because it's obviously being wasted on me.
All I have to say to that is, "bullshit."

Nat thinks I should star in pornographic films
(and he's serious).
I reply, "I'm much too old for that."
Nat says it hasn't been a problem for him,
but I think that's bullshit.

Nat says he can tell by looking at me
that I hang to the right;
that I blindly nod my head
when quantum mechanics are discussed,
and secretly have a crush on Johnny Depp.
I insist that that's bullshit,
but come to think of it,
Johnny Depp is pretty dang cute.

Nat says that my inordinate fear of Jell-O molds is
Freudian in nature and
can be directly associated to the time that
Shriner clown made me pull his finger.

Nat says that what he's just set on the plate before me
is succulent cow pie.
I say it's bullshit.

Sarah at the Coliseum (for Sarah McKinstry-Brown)

Friends, Romans, put down your beers.
I stand here before you with a story of great import.
'Tis a telling of heroic proportion…nay, legend.

Visualize if you will, the Coliseum.
A Coliseum soaked not with blood, but with hooch.
Yes, hooch.
Booze. Suds. Liquor. Libation.
Alcohol if you will.
Take a hit. Cannonball that.
The next warrior is about to enter the arena.
Kick an empty beer bottle across the floor.
Ah…Now that's poetry.
Sling a thousand bottles down the Coliseum's steps.
That's a proper fanfare.
Yes, and there amidst the din of shattered glass…
Listen.
For lo, but beneath earthy floorboards
you can hear the roar of the beasts,
and how they bellow for more spilt pilsner!

And now,
out from the ranks of
our downed and vanquished gladiators,
A chant arises.
"Sarah. Sarah. Sarah."
[And at this point,
the narrator is forced to interject with, "Sarah?
What the heck kinda'
name for a warrior is that?"
Never-mind.]
Yes.
The games call for another victim.
And yet
there is no victim.
What you have here is the deadliest of poet warriors.
No mere bone cruncher, but poem cruncher.
Her words are sharp.
Her verse heavy as a lead mace.
Yeah, but she strides forward into the arena and
an ocean of ankle deep lager rises to part before her.
Her armor of choice is unusual.

Yes, sports fans.
Today Sarah appears to have chosen
an oversized knit cardigan,
and beneath that, low-cut denim jeans
with just a hint of a dark t-shirt.
Menacing stuff indeed,
but such sinister fashion
has been lost on the inebriated masses.
Perhaps this nondescript apparel
was designed to make her appear invisible.
Indeed, though her fellow gladiators
know of her presence all too well,
to the drunken hordes arrayed about the coliseum,
she is persona non grata.

No matter.
Sarah circles around to square off
before an archaic microphone circa 2003 BC,
and settling into a broad stance,
words begin to dart forth and thrust outward.
Where all previous poet combatants had chosen
bludgeoning verbiage via heavy bladed broadsword,
Sarah's attack comes by way of exquisite rapier.
Its shimmering surface
projects a vocal glissade out to the arena's far reaches.
Indeed, there at the back of the Coliseum,
one of the inebriated spectators pauses
mid broken bottle to ocular socket and remarks,
"Hey dude! She's talkin' 'bout sex!"

Yes. Oh, Yes.
Sarah's talkin' 'bout sex.
The punters way up in the bleachers
ease back their oral fixation
upon long neck liquid phallus'
and rack bleary eyes
towards the lethal siren behind the microphone.
The murmur from the back row sweeps forward.

"Sex?
Oh yes. Sex good.
Sex is our friend.
We like sex."

Yes. Sarah's talkin' 'bout sex, but hey!
This ain't a dirty poem.
Hell, the dirty poems are up in the bleachers.
Oh yea, and also what's going on
underneath that table right there.
No. Sarah's serving up clean sex.
Keen edged clean sex that
skewers the soft pink eardrums of
each and every booze binging Roman.
Um…
Except, you know,
for those there distracted beneath that table.

A poetic martial art,
her wordsmith utterances slither forth
to slice Roman cerebellum with
double edged XY chromosome.
Yes. If Sarah bleeds, she bleeds pure estrogen.
An estrogen of such might that it vanquishes every
testosterone laced,
booze braced poet
who ever preceded her.
And then…
And then some blotto Roman
pulls his thumb from his waistband,
raises it above the table before him
and wraps it around the lip of a longneck Budweiser.
With this, one hundred thousand toga attired
bacchanalian sots follow suit.

Yes. For a few seconds, poetry rolled forth over
the entire tanked up Roman empire.
For a few seconds, culture and civilization reigned.

For a few seconds…
Then some drunken idiot in the back
got out his fiddle, started to play,
and the lady at the mic was swept away to oblivion.
Rome may be burning, but what the fuck.
Put another keg on the tap.
Bring another poet to the slaughter.
Sarah
has left
the building.

The Poem

The poem that rocked the world.
The poem that exploded
and changed everything as we know it.
It doesn't exist.
It doesn't exist except in your head.
Yes, right there in every poet's unique, individual head.
What? You thought you had something of relevance to say?
You thought some hill tribesman in upper Cambodia
was going to swoon at your poetic remembrance of one
particularly passionate night
in the backseat of you parent's car.
No. It doesn't touch him.
Doesn't touch his aunt either.
Neither of them care about how precisely you've described
the texture of a car's vinyl seat cover
against your sweaty naked backside.
So you're angry.
You write very, very angry poetry.
You've gone cutting edge political with your rant.
Ah, if the world could only hear your point of view.
Yea, but it's a poem.
A po-em.
You're a poet, and you write po-et-ry.
On your best day you stand at a microphone

in front of 25 people tops,
and half of those listening
are actually thinking about their own poem…
their own little "something of relevance."
Of those remaining,
your poem has already drained from their pre-packed ears,
off shoulder, and slithered to the ever waiting carpet.
If you're lucky, one person vaguely remembers your face,
though no one remembers your name.
So, the poem that rocked the world?
I guess it depends on the size of your world.
For me, I feel I've had a devastating impact up to
about three feet out from my body.
Beyond that point, I am nothing more than noise.
Background sound to that poem that's in your head right now.
You know…
The poem that's gonna rock the world.

JM Huscher

Inappropriate Behavior

When the storm hits
you run for shelter

that's why you are here, in my arms
because somewhere behind your eyelids it is raining
the flood is overflowing one drop at a time
down your rounded cheek and onto your chin
it burns like boiling water all the way down
but you don't wipe it away.
i do.

And this is not appropriate behavior for two straight men.

9 months ago I called you

and the news became as broken as I was
and there, in public, you held me

not a hug
you were embracing me
holding me together
containing me
your arms keeping guts in like a turnicate
your hands white-knucked around my back
and me leaving saline, saliva, and snot on your shoulder
because when men cry, it's not pretty
and me weak-kneed after a week of bleeding through my shirts
leaving stains in the shape of a woman's name
and we were attracting the attention of six lanes of traffic and two bus stops
public transportation patrons who couldn't help but think

This is not appropriate behavior for two straight men

but she broke me then.
emotional pain became physically actualized
and I could feel her
using the needle to inject her name into the left side of my chest
so that everytime my heart beat blood through capillaries
my entire body was filled with her memory
i could feel her leaving in my fingertips
it was like static discharge waiting to happen and I was
whincing for weeks
waiting for relief
but it hung on
like a short night's sleep
and you held me then.
but now it's my thumb doing the windshield wiper sweep across your cheek.

And this is not appropriate behavior for two straight men.

I'm here because your father isn't emotional enough
and your mother isn't strong enough
because each exhaled breath is a silent scream

and even inhaling feels like letting go
because it's a misconception
The presence of a Y chromosome does not inhibit emotion
You are in my arms because
I want you to know
that I don't give a fuck about anything or anybody but you right now.

And this is not appropriate behavior for two straight men

i become the incantation
the meditation
the slow rolling ohm
i am your prayer
and if the honesty of a plea translates to spiritual volume
then God can't hear anyone but me.
If I can't save your life
I will resurrect you

I would scream I love you
kiss you
and stand up to the flying rocks from old-school jocks
and chauvinists who believe they know more about man than God does
if I thought it would save you right now.
I would hold you until
until it's over.

this is not appropriate behavior for two straight men

but it fucking should be

Unpicturesque

Tonight I am looking at the pictures
that didn't come out

like the one we took in St. Louis
at the top of the arch

I look like I'm on enough morphine
to kill a small child.
You look like you're boiling over
angry
and livid
like you just found out that I'm on enough morphine
to kill a small child.

The stranger holding my camera urged us to retake
and in the second shot
we look beautiful
perfect smile
perfect light
perfect posture
perfect arms around me just right

and that *first* photograph got put away
because we want to remember our *first*
vacation together
using words and pictures that describe
what it was not
See, I would rather forget about
the fourth night of that trip
when our words became verbal cutlery
when I said,
"I don't think I know you at all."
Then you put my precarious admission
in your mouth
chewed it up and spat it out.

Unintentionally,
unknowingly
we verbally
cut and uncut
until our blood
painted the floor
And
we

were
desperate
and we were hanging on by white fingertips
if we were even hanging on at all.
And we did not look like anything
that second photograph

So I can't afford to recall those days
as the scenic smiles of a couple that looks great
everywhere
all the time
The truth is that's not who we were
and it's not who we are

we often presuppose that the good memories
are the only ones worth keeping
(the photograph where you aren't blinking.)
why do we pretend
that we need to forget
how fucked up things can be and have been?

I need the photographs your mother hasn't seen
and that will never be framed
and that we'd just assume
never
even
happened

Why?
because in
and in
spite of
our unpicturesque moments
especially those not caught on film
We are still together
unintentioally winking
or with red-eye, slouching, in bad lighting, blurry,
with the top of our heads cut off

or with the lens cap still on
we are still together

Tonight I would tell you that I love you
If I thought it would make a difference

But I don't know that I do
And I don't know that it would

And we are hanging on by white fingertips
if we are even hanging on at all.
and maybe we're only together
because I am afraid of being alone.

Tonight, I know that we're not perfect
or maybe we're not even good
but I just needed to remember
that we're still in these shitty photographs

together.

It Only Works If You Empathize

This is a love poem
and I'm not reciting it for anyone but you
even if I read it in a room full of
strangers I haven't yet, won't, or don't want to meet
I'm reading it for you
and you know who you are.

You, who woke up beside me
shaking me awake to remind me of invading armies
battalions of the minutes, moments, hours, seconds of everyday life
I killed them off one-by-one
I told them to go fuck themselves
because no day is an everyday when you're with someone.

You, who allowed me to appear as if I had it together,
because real men don't cry
Men don't really cry
Don't all men really cry?

and it's still
You, with him
and
You, who asked me to give you space

I would insert-over-the-top-physically-impossible-romantic-cliche-here for you.
I would swim oceans, climb mountains, ford rivers, kill armies, and eat beef for
you
A whole 16 oz. sirloin, bloody enough that if you listen close enough
you can still hear it moo.

but you asked me to give you space, and it's the only thing I don't want to give
you.
When I said I'd swim the deepest ocean, I thought I'd be swimming toward you.

I guess this is you
finding out whether I'd rather have you
happy with someone else
or unhappy with me
and goddamnit if I don't really want the second one

but I guess this is you
finding out whether I love you or I love me
and maybe you don't even give a fuck
but I'm proving it anyway

So I'll give you space that would make all of Nasa blush
I'm give you time that would make Rolex give up.
and I'd like to make a suggestion as well

Nobody came to hear love poetry
We want that political shit
tired recycled and rehearsed verse about Dubya, Rumsfeld, and the CIA

or that funny stuff Dan Leamen does
it's cute as a bug
in a rug
until he mentions masturbation

Love poetry only works if you empathize
so you could help me out
by breaking his fucking heart like you did mine.
then HE could sit in the front row and yell "FUCK YEAH!" when I finish this
poem.

You're not even here right now
but I'm putting all of this out there.
into the oxygen in front of me
because I know that you are somewhere you are inhaling air
and maybe you'll breath this in
and my syllables will hit your lungs, join your blood
and find the way to your heart that I never could

The last line of this poem should have been "I love you," but you're not here to
hear it, so it ended like this.

Melissa A. Kandido

Blue Thursday

He tried to justify these black eyes/blue tears/the red blood flooding my insides
Justify the color of hurt,
Just if I would leave this drastic rainbow of make-up painted faces
Covering up traces of shame with the blush of self-blame.
Covering up the evil that masquerades as good
I'm ready to trade in these concussions
From playing Russian roulette with a person whose loaded
With semi-automatic rage
I stare down the barrel of a gun when I look in his eyes
And I wonder how the rule of "thumb" was from history when

Men were not allowed to beat women with anything
longer than their hitchhiking finger.
He lays more than fingers on me,
I live at the hands of a man
Hands that hurt instead of hold
Hands that scar more than skin, they wound my dreams
And my soul screams to wake up my mind
Because love might be blind
But my other senses do not fail me and
Feet don't fail me now
Cuz I'm running
I'm running
I'm running
Out of his cunning cycle
Out of this house
Because this all hits home
Hit me, bit me, tripped me
Made these episodes skip repeatedly
Like a bad record with scratches, he
Split my eyes that were knitted with stitches,
The careful design in the art of abuse
Drastic denial with emotional evasiveness
Subtle psychological games played in this
Vicious verbal battery
Recharged when I kept coming back like
Bad sequel movies
Keep coming back running in ring-around the roses
You gave me to make up for the rings around my eyes
Kept coming back like a baseball player running the bases—
Hey batter-batter—
Hey batter-batter—
Swing, batter!
Batterer kept me coming back to the shelter
But now I'm running helter skelter
Cuz I am that woman
The one they talk about
In whispers,
"I heard he took a belt to her."

"I heard she carried ice packs in coolers in her car."
"I heard her through the walls and he hit her hard!"
Brutal beatings that kept me
clinging to the edge of a cliff 24 hours a day
Tiptoeing through the house so I didn't wake his rage.
But you wounded my fetus
And I won't let you beat us anymore,
So like the song said,
Kiss me and I'll kiss you back—
Smack me and I'll smack you back
And now I'm back from black eyes/blue tears/the red blood

Bruce Koborg

Chicago Spook-a-Rama

"You're not a poet! You're just a BUM! With CHAPBOOKS!"
—Nat Derickson.

"Heya, Mr. Rock Star Poet, whatcha doin' here? And whennarya goin' back?"
—Sherman Alexie—sort of.

Can I get on your mailing list?
How much is your CD?
Will you sign it—for me?
I want—
Your website.
Will you write something—for me?
Will you read my stuff?
To what, shall we compare thee to a summer's day? Or some such other thinly
plagiarized fraud.
Leading the revolution from the safety of an undisclosed coffee house. Get a Job?
Are you kidding me?
Roll out of the rack before noon?
Singin' the same tune for the last 10 years,
Black clothed and Hot Topic tagged,

Bono glasses for the masses,
This champion of the working classes, with soft hands and fat ass,
Never dug out retaining walls, never puddled concrete,
But, has taken classes to be a hip hop hipster,
Trippin lip fork tongue spouter of bullshit.
Rymin' schemin, I'm my own teamin', trashy flashy, gimme some of your cashy,
cause the points aren't the point,
I AM the point!
My words will help you see that I am the truth
And the way.
And I'll write you a piece for a piece,
and I've got parties to get invited to,
Because, "If I eat, then you eat."
It's just a matter of time before we meet.

How Nat Derickson brought me over to the "Dark Side"

Way back in 2003, Omaha sent its first official team to Slam Nationals in Chicago. People from Omaha had participated before, but as individuals and as members of other teams. Matt Mason and Sara Lihz were on the Des Moines team previously, Sarah McKinstry-Brown had been there with Albuquerque, Bad Andy had been there with Memphis, only Dominique Garay and Jim Morrison were newcomers, but you wouldn't know it by watching them perform.

The Chopin Theatre in Wicker Park served as the primary venue for the National Slam that year. The carnival-like throng in the lobby and outside the doors of Chopin Theatre consistently had a few performers exchanging cigarettes and contact information, flogging their CDs and chapbooks, and speculating as to which team would advance. It was a cross between March Madness and a political convention. For once, the performance poets were out in force; no longer were they relegated to the nether regions of their local coffee shops, they quickly, and inevitably, formed their own social order. Teams from the bay area, New York, or Chicago, dominated the discussion. It was expected that they would advance to the final four, much like Duke University can be counted on to be a finalist in a basketball tournament. To continue the basketball analogy, it was as if the other teams were to play the role of the 'Washington Generals' in a Harlem Globetrotters exhibition game.

On the periphery of the competition, there were a host of events somewhat associated with the Slam competition; one of which, was a daily open mike at Phyllis' Musical Inn a couple of blocks from the Chopin Theatre. Nat Derickson and I had traveled with the team, partly out of curiosity of what Nationals were all about and partly so we could share a cheap motel room. We had seen many of the celebrated performance poets and teams and we realized that our team had better and more original writers, and they were as good as anybody else when it came to performance. After one particularly ugly event involving an Anti-War Open Mike—the sign up resembling a cross between a shark feeding frenzy and the scene from 'On the Waterfront' where the longshoremen fight over the token that will allow them to work for the day—Nat and I thought it best to go find some beer.

Below the Old Style Beer sign, we found Phyliss' Musical Inn, home of the open mike reading and social hour. A couple of 'rock star poets' came in, did their poems by rote, got emotional, cried on cue, and then tried to shake down various audience members to buy their chapbooks, or buy them beer, etc. We returned for more of the same the following days. Then on Thursday or Friday of that week, the open mike was set up to be out in Phyliss' patio/beer garden outside. As with many poetry events, 5:00 came and there was no sign up sheet nor a host for this event; 5:10 came, members of the Pittsburgh team arrived and wanted to know who was running the show. Since nobody else was doing it, Nat went up to the 'stage' area and began the festivities. A German poet started off, we couldn't understand a word he said, but we knew he was a slammer from his delivery. He came all this way just to be part of this event. He didn't give a crap about who won, or the points, or who sold the most chapbooks. He reminded about 20 people in that courtyard why they got started in poetry. For about an hour, until the neighbors complained about the noise and we were shut down, we shared a real open mike. No sign ups, just each poet taking their turn, building upon the person who came before, it was like a jam session of spoken word. A moment where we cheered the Pittsburgh team, they cheered for us, and the points just didn't matter anymore.

Angie Kritenbrink

69340

a series of petty crimes and tragic accidents
imprisoned me in this cubicle.

seasons come and go
suns rise and fall, but these beige walls
keep me from knowing when

I forget what month it is

I cling to my radio,
NPR my only lifeline
Son Volt, Le Tigre,
Ani DiFranco in my headphones

voices no one else can hear
reminding me not to get comfortable here
among the soft tap tap tapping of keyboards,
health benefits and regular lunch schedules

my thoughts run in circles
they have no place to go
these walls are getting closer, closer

We start going to meetings
where they talk about rising health care costs
and "government interference" in the business,
revamping our public image, trying to stay competitive.

I write inspiring quotes
on the markerboard they gave me
for meeting quality in September of 2001,
or June of 99, or December of 98,
I don't know,

I don't know what year it is

they are purchasing my soul by the hour
twelve dollars at a time.

I am summoned to a one-on-one meeting
where it is explained to me that my footwear is
Inappropriate Business Attire.
There Have Been Complaints,
I am told.

I want to fuck the guy in the cube next to me
even though he has a finance degree
and wears the same plaid shirt to the bar every time I see him.

I want to stand up,
watch all their heads pop up over the cube walls
as I scream:

You do not own me
I am not machinery
You can not put a number on my soul

But that would be against the Code of Conduct.

so I get them to pay for a bachelor's degree
while I pay everything they give me to deny

and then I bust out and start running.

and I am tired, I am still racing, still paying penance,
but my thoughts go in straight lines now,
and I am getting some sun,
and I am getting somewhere.

homegirl

I know how to fly
down gravel roads, while birds rise
from bushes and tree-lined creek beds,
riding clouds of dust up, up, catching a breeze
settling a few cornfields over, fluttering wings
disappearing in a sea of green waves
rising and falling.

I've worked those fields for minimum wage,
served coffee to the men who planted them,
drank beer with them after baptisms,
whiskey at their fall weddings.

I knew I'd have a bachelor's degree by thirty,
but I'd wanted to have babies first.

I enjoy housework:
the smell of fresh laundry,
the ordering of clean things
stirring the dust around and vacuuming it up.

I've lived in impermanent cities,
where you can still feel the wind from the prairies,
green cities near rivers that still show their strength,
green skies in summer threatening
these air-conditioned toothpick houses we live in.

Now twenty-nine, living alone with a farm cat
I can't quite civilize, I'm starting on a master's degree,
then thinking about Iowa City,
or Colorado, or Boston, or Lincoln.

Now mid-July, living in an upstairs mid-town apartment
I'm hungry for tomato sandwiches,
fried eggs with crispy edges and runny yolks,
toast from the freezer, orange juice from concentrate,

black mud under my red painted toenails,
ninety degree sun on my face, I miss
the smell of lake water in my hair
as I rest in a beach chair, reading:

the only escape I ever need.

Dan Leamen

Firefly

I spend tonight as alone as a fire fly
flashing like a heartbeat gone neon
and dancing against the backdrop of a starless sky.
And I don't feel so dizzy weavnig
an unconcious shoestring path around a giant
that's not there.
I am ridiculously without a partner,
and can't manage to make it look like I know the steps,
but this is not a love poem.
But, aren't all poems love poems?
Words half tempted to close their eyes and pretend,
this is a story,
is a firefly turning the gun on its abdomen,
blowing its diamonds for guts
into oblivion,
planting stars in the starless night
to tell the story of us.
And I know that sounds ridiculous.
But there's a story in the sky.
And why can't it be ours?
Senses gone nova sending memories
to secret places of oblivion
so that when lover's search for the constellation of us
they will realize love is sometimes not perfect,

just a beautiful story.
And here we are again
arguing over us again
me wanting you to pull the trigger again,
flying wads of sparkle into the starless forever,
so I know that there is an us
to tell this story about.
But, you just walk away again,
leaving us at almost again,
leaving me choking on a neon poem…
Your eyelashes are cliff edges
over which I commit suicide to search for your soul.
Somedays I think that's what it will take
to be born again,
to love again.
And I've decided there are two suns,
because two sunrises are the only things beautiful enough
to lift the corners of your mouth
into your smile.
And I whisper this poem just for you.
I am not a firefly,
but I play one in my dreams
where there are never starless nights
where giants keep tripping over their shoestrings
where fireflies speak in diamond tongues
where all the dancing I talk about
is done
with you.

Wal-Mart Poem Version 2

So it's 10:38 on a Tuesday morning
and I'm at my summer job—produce department at Wal-Mart.
It's busy, Tuesday morning busy,
which at, say a donut shop,
means there are six old dudes sipping coffee and reminiscing.
At Wal-Mart this means that the entire population of the midwest,

half of the eastern sea board, 17 people from california, four midgets from
the cast of Willow, three small dogs, the guy who played Luke Skwalker, and
an entire generation of unborn children are shopping.
I can't figure it out
Maybe they have come to pay homage to Sam Walton,
and our everday low prices,
drink Sam's Choice Pop laced with cyanide
in hopes of their souls joining Sam on a
Sam's Club trailing a comet heading toward
the eternal land of Wal-Mart people greeters and
bargain bin Jackie Chan movies.
But, I know the truth, these people are here to visit me,
the oracle of Wal-Mart
and pose deeply philosophical questions, such as:
'Can you talk to buyer? I used to eat an orange a day and now they are
fifty cents a piece.'
To which I respond, 'Yes sir,
I, Dan, stocker of broccoli and filler of cantaloupe bins,
armed with my one day use produce apron and size large latex gloves
can call up our buyer and tell him to get some freakin' cheaper oranges.'
As I finish one answer another question
clips me at the knee,
'Young man, do you have a grocery section?'
'Nope, sorry ma'am, the only grocery section we have
is the one you're standing in.'
Then, 'Can you pick me out a good watermelon?'
and, 'I'm looking for these dried tomatoes.
No, not those. These are in a little jar shaped like a stop sign.'
The world of customer service is guns blazing.
We have no defense and could use some kids with sling shots
or a mote
or a mote full of kids with sling shots,
but no people would still come.
We could post signs stating that anyone who enters will be executed by a
Delta Force sniper squad.
We could blare over the intercom that God is in Wal-Mart
handing out the bad side of the apocalypse -
'Attention Wal-Mart customers, Jesus is handing out plague, and fire and

brimstone. But until he renders judgment on your eternal souls we'll be
serving hot fresh french bread in the bakery. Thank you for shopping at
what is soon to be the seventh circle of hell biatches.'
But still people will pour in.
And for what, to hang out?
Wal-Mart's not cool like that.
So this is what I've got to say to you Wal-Mart:
You are a dirty, dirty punk
and if I had a rock I'd throw it at your knee cap
and if I had two dollars I'd shop somewhere else,
so, here, guy who has nothing to do on Tuesday morning
take my one day use apron I'm going to fucking Target.

Give (a. k. a Love Poem)

Give words with a poetry back gurantee.
Give words that become the air we breathe before we fall asleep,
Give words like the puff of smoke
soul your body will leave behind
to cystalize and become birds
like carrier pigeons
carrying words
between beats of hearts
where there is space and time
and life and love are not sure about coming back
and all you can do is feel…
alive.
Then slide 'cut' and 'razor' like you're all alone like suicide
in between their letters to discover
poetry,
like doing the robot we you shouldn't
giving love when she wouldn't
like dialing the number of a person you don't know
and talking to them for hours
like waltzing whispers of 'I love you' that rise above the breath.
Poetry,
wrapped in smiles and frowns and open like lips in kiss

to be performed.
To give you the extremes and rewind the in-betweens.
To deliver a fist full of alphabet from throat to ear
making you gasp in happiness
and gasp in prayer, because
the mic deserves such splendor.
Deserves a thousand shooting star-words in a soft under siege,
like mouths filled with flowers,
with lions,
with I imagine your skin is as smooth as the space between the stars,
with
unwind the diatribe like shedding skin
and drop your lips and ears to the ground so you may travel the
people pulse like ocean currents
and keep your lips kissing the earth of home and
your ear to the microphone,
because the mic is the beat box for anything.
Words slipping between hip and hop.
Words slipping between silence and applause. Between
crescendos and decrescendos like the cosmos is colliding with itself
and words are sorting it all out. Like
words are making the stage an evaporating floor of feathers
where transcendence becomes an action—not a state of mind.
Give yourself to make a crowd of 1 rock like 70,000.
Give your words to leave a world full of language chasing breath
like everyone exhaled.
Put your eyes into your voice and your voice into the mic
and speak.
I wrote this poem because we are
all walking,
down streets of hearts
like spring days and sunrises are blooming
beneath our rib cage.
Like rain is falling in lungs,
Like our souls are crucified christmas presents.
So when you stroll pass
that empty hat on the sidewalk
don't give dollars and dimes.

You have a gift.
Give love.
Give laughter.
and at anytime
give poetry.

Sara Libz

Poem for a Monday

Walking down 60th and Benton you'd think
she doesn't see it. You can't get smiles
like that from girls like her on dirty streets
with broken houses, shambles for homes.
Walking down 60th and Benton she sees
everything and smiles.

The happiest girl you've ever met saw your face
on a bad day; full of stress and acne;
full of annoyance at the rain as you walk
to your "for now" job. As you walk and
"Hey!" She grabs your hand. Unafraid
of a stranger stops you both in the rain to say
"You are so beautiful."
Her voice full of surprise and awe. If you let her
she will call you everyday just to tell you
how beautiful you are. If you try
you will never doubt her sincerity.

The giddiest girl you ever saw can talk
circles around the politics you follow like it's
election year.
Understands better than you do why you registered
Republican.
Why you keep voting Democrat.
She buys a newspaper every day; reads the whole thing

but refuses
to subscribe and have it delivered. Refuses to be
political.
Refuses to discuss it
for more than an hour a week.

So that's one hour to politics. One hour
to hot bathes. One hour to poetry
and six hours to strangers.
Random ones. Grocery store strangers
and little girl strangers. She shops in strange places
just to meet them. Comes home exhausted to throw
surprise parties even though it's no one's birthday;
even though no one is prepared. She just wants
the shock of it. Wants someone's tears
from the thought of it; of someone thinking about them
for no particular reason.

The sweetest girl you've ever encountered cries
at least once a day. But only when no one's looking.
But only to water her eyelashes. She'll smile
the whole half hour and she'll smile brighter
when she's through and she'll give that smile to you.
With a tug on your hand and hug
on your way she will give it all away

because walking down 60th and Benton
it's all she has to give.
Smile so big you'd think she doesn't see it.
Smile so big you'd think she's stupid.
Smile so big you're amazed at her ability to see
beauty in everything.
But there is no beauty here. Sewage backed up
so bad it's coming around
from the backs of houses. Basements boarded off.
Occupants returning only because there's nowhere
else to go. No. There is no beauty here.
Even she will tell you that.

But walking down 60th and Benton she smiles
bright and wide. Some days,
Some days she'll walk it twice
just to be sure she's done all she can.

The Undefeated

Like the eruption of Mt. St. Helen's in 1980,
we rearranged the world to make room for us;
nestled ourselves into the crook of a cornfield,
and ran that field rampant letting our dust
paint the sky red for months.

But lately, we lock eyes over breakfast and move
to introduce ourselves. We argue over our folly,
but this pale face shaking is a white flag waving.

When we first met, we aligned our borders and locked
our fingers like Pangea. And when the impossible
happened,
when the earth shook itself awake to rearrange its
mountains, I could still feel
you; cradled against the river that ran along my back.

From several cities away I would sneeze as my phone
rang
and you called to say "Gesundheit."

But the river that cushioned our distance has turned
into an ocean. Didn't you're mother ever tell you?
Love is a fresh water fish. So when we wind up on
separate plates,
borders scraped raw from fighting the change,
you can stop trying to draw maps of the fault
lines running through our history, because if
continents

can move apart through no fault of their own,
then so can we. We are not lost.
We are Persephone and Hades.
I've been waiting for Spring.

Accents of a Grandfather

At 18 years old she begins to learn
that independence is a struggle.
She shares bunk-beds with a stranger, finds
the hardest part is not in what they share
but what separates them.

Her roommate's fear of anything east of 45th street
and south of Martha makes it nearly impossible
for near strangers to understand why she finds
comfort in bilingual sale signs hanging
en ventanas de tiendas
where todos los dias,
everyday, is take your child to work day.

Nearing the holidays, now much closer
than strangers, people begin swapping stories,
trading traditions, packing dorm-mates into backseats
so everyone gets a Christmas.

She's taking home two
suitcases of dirty laundry.

It's not that she didn't offer,
but people couldn't understand
why her primarily German family
eats enchiladas y mole for Christmas dinner.

And those with similar traditions
couldn't understand why she and her sisters
grew up as muchachitas,

and how she, more than any of the others,
knew that "Venga! Pronto!"
was a syllable shy of a slap in the face.

She grew up with these words, this language,
knows it like the flavor of Mamon Chino,
She can taste the fruit but can't describe it.

Understand it is a fair and beautiful language,
but it's meant for a background oscuro
and against her pale European features
the letters blend and merge; her tongue
swells and stumbles over the sounds
pronouncing only a fraction of what she's trying to
say.
Just because she cannot force the words aloud
doesn't mean she doesn't know their sound,
rhythm and meaning as well as the English
that flows so eloquently from her lips.

She wishes she could explain it all in Spanish,
translate to English,

But her words are telling the stories she was told
as a child by her German-Mexican grandfather,
about fleeing Chihuahua during the civil war,
about hiding in boxcars and watching
his home burn. Telling the stories
that neither of them can tell in anything
but broken English.

Matt Mason

Code Orange

"There are known knowns. These are things we know that we know. There are known unknowns. That is to say, there are things that we know we don't know. But there are also unknown unknowns. There are things we don't know we don't know."

> —Secretary of Defense Donald Rumsfeld clarifying US policy on the war on terror at a Department of Defense News Briefing

It
's not always
the little boy
who cries
Wolf!
sometimes
the wolf
cries
wolf

and
points   away.

Duct tape your doors shut,
we're on Code Orange, Code Orange, people,
blue skies
no matter, there's anthrax
somewhere, somebody said something about smallpox
wherever, an unnamed man reportedly said something
big
was coming down
eventually. The man said
people were going to die,
people are going to die,
Americans are going to die.

Officials are quoted as saying things,
officials are quoted as saying, Hurry, hurry, run,
seal yourself in a ziplock bag
in a lead-walled box
in a hole
in the earth
in prayer to our God,

and sources report
we aren't ready, we're not scared enough
and if we don't get a little more hysterical,
then the terrorists will win

because sources suggest
it could be any day, hour, minute, second,
duck!
it could be any metropolis, city, small town, farmstead,
or possibly even somewhere else; for God's sake,
there are
experts
saying
we're not safe, we're not safe,
now do what we say
and nobody gets hurt.

There's fear
out past your walls, there's fear itself
blowing against the plastic sheeting and the bars of grey tape,
there's so much
to fear, we must do more,
we have to fight them,
kill them, cripple them
for Jesus,
        Amen!

It's not always
the little boy
who cries

Wolf!
Sometimes the wolf
cries wolf.

And it's not always the wolf
our little boys are sent out
to kill.

[previously published: *From Page to Stage and Back Again*, Wordsmith Press and
It's 478 Miles To Chicago, Morpo Press]

The Baby That Ate Cincinnati

—Dedicated to those others who on telling people you're expecting your
first child find they don't say "Congratulations," they first tell you how
you're never leaving the house again, ever.

Way they say it,
they say
            baby
like a storm on the way,
they say   baby
like that's the cue for the thunderclap
to interrupt the wolves' long howls,
they say   I got three
and they're the best
ever happen to me
as they say
            baby
same as you'd say "run"
they shout
            baby
like there are flames lickin' at window frames

    tell us
    how their lives
    didn't just change,

oh no,

as
they
say
                    baby
like a hyena inside there
comin' out fangs a-blazin',
they say
                    baby
like it's standing
right
behind us
like it's a tornado on the highway,
                         but ain't
            it
            a marvel,

way they talk,
give that patronizing nod
when we
claim we still goin' to poetry readings,
we still goin' to see movies,
we still goin'
to phone our unwed friends
as they say
                    baby
like a bomb in the air,
they say
                    baby
like just waitin' in the shelter now
with AM radio and a can of pork n' beans

                    you're so lucky,
they weep,
sincerely

as I sit on the bed,

knees held precious,
watching my wife's belly,
larger every day,
wonderin'
what's in there.

We gonna need a priest, a gun,
silver bullets, wire cutters, 16 gallons a hydrochloric acid,
Red Cross, National Guard, seven million dollars
in non-sequential unmarked bills
because all these warnings giftwrapped with blessings
when   I   know

ain't gonna be the same around here;
but

baby,

when we say "baby,"
let's say it
like "bread,"
like "honey,"
like "beautiful,"
like "dear,"
like it's true.

[previously published: *402/NE-POETS,* Morpo Press]

The Good News

"Tell the good news about Jesus"

—a bumper sticker I followed for a long time

Jesus lent me ten bucks when I forgot my wallet at lunch.
Sure, he could've ordered a chicken pesto sandwich
and broke it into two full meals, but he's no show off.
That's what I like about Jesus.

Jesus listens to cool music. If it weren't for Jesus,
I never would have known about Tom Waits
or Ani DiFranco, and I sure wouldn't own any Lyle Lovett.
But Jesus makes a kickass mix tape.

Jesus loves cows,
thinks my poems with cows in them are a hoot
and encourages me
to look at herds of white cows
in a green field
and imagine salvation
is underneath each windmill.

Jesus tells me Pat Robertson's right,
and so is Al Sharpton.
That they're both wrong, too,
but that's not the point.
His point's how God's sewn into every fabric.
Even yourself. Even Elvis.

Jesus saves and Jesus recycles.

Jesus eats fish for more
than Omega-3 fatty acids,
drinks red wine for more reasons
than his sacred heart.

Jesus doesn't dress like the Medieval paintings
with the gold hats and the Mr. T rosaries.
Sure, he can clean up nice,
but Jesus likes blue jeans.

Jesus pisses me off
with his honesty
sometimes.
But it's not like he's ever wrong.

Jesus makes a killer chianti,
but he refuses to turn water
into Diet Coke for me.
"What's the difference?" he asks.

Jesus acts real serious
when somebody rushes up to him hollering, "Jesus,
can you take me up to Heaven,
I will see you in the Kingdom, Jesus!"
Jesus says they should get their kumbayayas off
by putting on some overalls
and hammering in the morning.
May as well make Heaven bigger,
not just your egos.

Jesus digs the "How does Jesus eat M&M's" joke.
He won't do it at a party, but he did do it once
when just the two of us were watching cartoons.

Jesus wanted me to tell you he loves you.
Jesus also wants you to stop doing that thing.

Jesus tells me I'm saved.
Then he laughs real loud.
Jesus makes me nervous when he does that.

[previously published: *Red, White, Blue*, Morpo Press]

Amy McGeorge

my misunderstanding with expandable panel pants and my three older sisters

I am the baby of my family.
The only one without children,

ex-husbands or current husbands
Free from the bonds
of marital bliss or unbliss
and childbirth,
I consider myself lucky.
But nights like this I am helpless
as my sisters spew forth
tales of pregnancy woes and worries
and rub my oldest sister's belly.
"Isn't it exciting?!" they say.
As if it is the single greates joy
of my life to discover that someday
I too may enjoy the wonder of childbirth
armed with the knowledge that
all of my sisters got big zits,
huge boobs,
swollen feet,
and an unsunny disposition.
What delight it brings me to know
I too can lie on my back,
feet in stirrups
with twenty strangers poking their heads
in and out of my crotch shouting,
"Oh yeah! She's up to six!"
and for some reason they bring in that
twenty-first person just so he can say,
"Oh yeah! She's up to six all right!"
HOT DAMN!

And my sisters discuss instruments.
Instruments that look like
knitting needles,
and tongs,
and forks,
and knives,
and plungers.
All this unnecessary information
makes my uterus hurt.

And I am reminded about the time
in 8th grade health class when my teacher
stood in front of the class
her arms in the air
her hands in fists
making a giant Y with her body
saying" These are the ovaries
These are the oviducts,
I am the uterus
and this is the vagina,"
and I blush all over again.

I want only to be the fun aunt.
The one who never tells my nieces and nephews no.
The one who hides them from mothers foaming at the mouth with anger,
the one who goes to India with her new
French boyfriend, Jean-Paul
and brings them back incense and little gold idols.
The cool bohemian aunt with long hair and ten cats.
And while my sisters drone on about water breaking,
fat bellies, sailor collar shirts and
pants with an expandable panel,
my neice Abby comes and sits on my lap—
holds my hand
looks at me with her lovely blue eyes.
"I love you Aunt Mayme.
Can we go outside?"
And we go play TV tag with her cousin Alex
screaming
Flintstones
Scooby Doo
Rug Rats
running, laughing, falling and skipping
till the porch light comes on.
And for a moment…
a brief flashing moment
I understand my sisters.

I understand it all
and my belly feels empty.

Black Cats

My father loved the Fourth of July—
the sound of black cats bursting in the distance,
gunpoweder and paper smoke thick in his nostrils.
He was ready to light up bottle rockets
in May, and by June the itch
was so strong he'd sneak out after supper
to smoke and set free one small rocket
scaring the dijm night sky with a single wisp of gray.

My mother, forever annoyed by the danger,
encouraged her four small daughters
to celebrate the holiday with caution—
we could lose a finger, or a toe,
and tehre was always the threat of blindness;
and although she fretted and warned,
you could find her sitting on the back porch
watching the sparks with a shimmer of quilty pleasure
a lit punk in her hand ready to assist.

Together as a family,
we would twist and tie one-and-a-half inchers
creating the world's greatest dog turd disposer,
Placing them into the center
of the piles of our black lab's poop.
Running far and fast as the short fuse
made its way down to the powder—
a boom/splat/boom that delighted us all—
except for the dog.

And when my father discovered M-80's,
my mother finally got rid of her broken canister vaccuum.
A colorful display of metal, tubes, dust and stupidity,

my father running with a cigarette in his mouth, yelling,
"Hit the deck, girls! Hit the deck!"
But no one go hurt and we lived to add
more punk burns to our knees.

Now far removed
from days of sun and smoke,
I breathe in the summer air and search
for signs of light in the night sky,
each bottle rocket a quick, short trail
back to when the explosions of laughter
outweighed the sounds of disintegration.

Grizz McIntosh

West of the 100th Meridian

—*after a visit to Fort Robinson*

Innocent blue eyes at the kiosk
inform us it was an accident, but we know Crazy Horse
was assassinated—sure as Lincoln or JFK—
in the name of Manifest Destiny.

Families are dumping RV chemical toilets
on the spot where Cheyennes starved for home—held
without water or heat in bitter Nebraska winter.

We debate who were savages and who
were civilized—counting coup on genocide.
Magpies scold us for intruding and we have no answers
for them or each other on this sinless June day.

I tap some tobacco out of a cigarette
next to the modest stone marking where Crazy Horse fell.
We study the barred windows that stopped him

in his tracks—that day and evermore.

I imagine dancing horses, tossing soft snorts
and whickers to fallen heroes and self-serve history.
I can hear kids playing in the RV park, unaware
that Dull Knife's group took desperate steps there.

With downcast minds, shamed by our *wasichu* blood
and its part in this old death, we watch a murder of crows
wheel as one and perform a fly-over—
like a county fair formation of Blue Angels.

Rural Routes

Maybe it was the Steve Earle on the tape deck
but Kooter fished the last handful
        of tens and twenties
out of the Hinky-Dinky sack and decided
it was time to liquefy their assets.
        She told Jack
to stop at the first neon sign for Coors.

They danced a sloppy two-step
        around truckers and cowboys
who only wanted to eat their noon cheeseburgers.
        Kooter smiled them all senseless
and traded a dance for a Carhartts jacket
        and a pair of fencing pliers.
She wore Jack's dented Stetson like a crown.

They drank the last bottle of beer
        and left the Dew Drop Inn behind.
They headed cross-country
        into the Sandhills,
cutting barbed-wire fences in the sunset
and leaving everything wide open.

Raging Slab

"Travellers, like poets, are a mostly angry race."
—Sir Richard Francis Burton

Gonna write gonzo poetry, flatout hauling outta
Lake Havasu, screaming all the way to Vegas.

Lead a group of wild-eyed poets on a ragged stanza
roadtrip across Amerika. Handpicked poets in tie-dyed

socks and leopardskin corsets, armed with bullhorns
and fresh batteries. Soap anarchist poetry on windshields

in new-car lots and shake our fists in elegy for Kerouac
and Cassady. Pour Niagara over our manifolds and ignite

fossilized brontosauri by the tankful, burn like Roman
candles—both ends flaming. Write sport utility poetry,

at home on pavement and dirt. Scribble off-road verse
on cocktail napkins—slip them into every motel Gideon

from coast to neon coast. Publish our own BurmaShave
verse in road ditches from Chicago to Santa Monica.

Vandalize forty-foot billboards with guerrilla poems
about trailer trash and evil monkeys, about gut-shot cows

and butt-dimpled chins. Burst across AM-FM static
quoting Ginsberg, Bukowksi and Hunter S. Thompson,

giving lions to Christians and fire to Philistines. Invade
every in-dash Philco and belt out twelve-bar wisdom

from Leiber & Stoller. Override all media outlets and flood
the airwaves with the chaotic musics of literate tongues.

Sarah McKinstry-Brown

In the Sixth Month

Your inner ear has fully formed.
You can hear now. I've heard
of mothers playing their unborn babies
the movements of Bach and Mozart
because studies show that classical music
makes the brain's spatial connections
arc towards one another like
the fingertips of Adam and God on the ceiling of the Sistine.

I've played no such music for you and maybe,
some day, when the boy you pine for
is majoring in architecture,
or when your brain goes cumulous and gray
as you stare at your pop quiz in geometry,
you will hold this against me.

Truth is, I cannot bear to wear headphones on my stomach
and force you to sit in the front row seat
of your mother the auditorium,
while Pachelbel's Canon fires off the synapses
of your brain, for the same reason I cannot bring myself
to have your father recite French
or fractions into my belly.

No sonata or tongue or equation could teach us
what we are learning already:
that to be human, is to be heavy,
to carry more than one heart inside of you.

Without speaking, you and I are two melodies
co-existing peacefully.
Israel and Palestine ought to blow up
their road maps and speeches and tanks,

put down their flags and put
their ears to my womb—
take notes on how our pulses negotiate,
listen to how this belly stretches like an accordion, a peace accord
making room for the song of you.

Transplant

I cut myself out of your landscape, Albuquerque,
because you thought you had me all mapped out. There
was no canyon or Village Inn, no major intersection
that didn't know where my fault lines rested.
So I packed my suitcase,
and let the longitude of my grief pull me
across the country.

Of course I missed you. At times it was hard to keep
breathing without your mountains around
to mirror the white crested peaks of my heartbeat.

I don't know if it was mistake or grace that brought me
here. When the Spaniards arrived in the New World,
their boot soles were heavy with dirt from the mother country.
This is how seeds of chickpeas and wheat made their way across the Atlantic

Maybe I arrived here via the soles of God's great invisible shoe.
Or maybe, I am more tumbleweed than free willed woman, maybe,
I docked into the arms of this city, my husband, by way of a careless wind.

Either way, it hasn't been easy to trade in the Rio Grande river
that rolled across your body like the Spanish rrrrr
on the tongue of a native New Mexican,
for the Missouri.

The flora of chile rellenos, frijoles, adobe,
the fauna of nightly tangos between police sirens and Mariachi,
don't grow here in farm country. But, Albuquerque,

have you ever seen a field of fireflies?
My first summer night on the plains,
I thought I was having a seizure or witnessing
the synapses of God's brain.
It was so beautiful I cried out.
And that's how it started—in the lungs,
it moved through the heart, went
to the liver, the joy spread
like a dandelion
until all my major organs
were playing a hymn inside the church
of this body. Albuquerque,
I'm going to stop talking now so you can listen
to the sound of a woman taking root in her skin.

Dropping Hints

The FBI is dusting book jackets for fingerprints,
their gloved hands man-handling a copy of
Tolstoy's Anna Karenina, looking for the prints of
a Communist,
a Leftist,
a Romantic.

When I'm not at the library,
I'm with you, Love:
leave an eyelash on your pillow;
strands of hair in your shower;
and when they leave my body,
my blue jeans are not in an undisclosed location—
they're right there at the base of your bed.

So if I keep writing all this anti-war poetry
and the FBI comes looking for me
they'd do well to check out a single, hardback copy of
you;
dust your skin as you sleep,

lift my lip prints from your cheek.

Turn the other one and I'm
tangoing again, with my laundry basket, my books, my computer
trying to get out of your front door and back to my apartment.
And if the FBI put a tap on this poem,
they'd trace it back to two minutes earlier
when I "accidentally" dropped my ring on your
bathroom floor.
We get to your car and you say, "do you have everything?" and I say
"I do."

For weeks, I wait in anticipation,
everything is infused with new meaning,
Even pigeon droppings on statues are beautiful,
become a thing to behold as I say,
"Honey, did you know those birds mate for life?"
And at night, when I look up at the stars,
my eyes following those breadcrumbs of light,
it seems plain as day we'll spend the rest of ours together.

Eventually you find my ring on your bathroom floor,
and trace it back to me—your footsteps follow you to my front door
And you ask, "Did you lose this?"
I say, "I do—
I mean, I did. I've been looking all over the place for that thing."

And if the FBI had any sense,
if the FBI had any capacity for feeling,
they'd stop dusting book jackets for fingerprints
they'd stop lifting ink-colored men out of airports.

I suspect that our situation is so grave,
I suspect that we've all been running laps around our fears
until even our own shadows are breaking into a sweat,
I suspect that Washington is pouring over maps of Iraq
while wedding dresses hang in windows,
I suspect that we are all blue in the face

corked tight like some fine red wine
because it's terrifying
in these times

to open up, to ask for things,
to say what we really mean.

We feed our imaginations bread and water,
sit back, cross our fingers, collect dust, look up to that guy on the cross
and imagine that nothing is up to us
as God and Fate arm-wrestle against the horizon.

But I've interrogated my heart and I'm turning myself in-
side out,
because this is a prayer
disguised as a poem
which is expressing an undercover desire to be your—
I do. I do.
Want you to be your, well you know—
no, you don't know:
I want to be your wife.

Michele Mitchell

i dont write love poems

i dont write love poems anymore
dont store sweet sentimate in sentences of simile
dont use imagery is describing the brilliance of your smile
while retelling tales of hours of touching, teasing, simultaneous pleasing

easing into a bliss so serene that breathing seems, to disturb it
im a poet
but i dont write love poems anymore
cuz words dont do you justice
there arent adjectives adequate enough

no verb,vivid
no noun nasty enough
to stratigically place in paragraphs to describe
what i see…
in the strength of your eyes, even when youre asleep
they keep asking me
but i dont write love poems anymore
i mean how could i scribe vibes that are evisioned
from exhales of ecstacy
from your hips
to my lips
i dont write love poems anymore
but if i did
i would take liquid gold and fold verses into egyptian silk
swathe the cloak over your magificence
and my poetry will decorate you like the royalty you are
i would snatch each moon
from each planet and mold them into one ominous star
then crush it into dust for your skin
so you would always glow
i would take yellow red and blue
mix them into different hues
so you could choose your rainbow
i would take the sun
into my grasp
and before you could i ask i would fill your heart with
warmth
light
and energy that i will live inside of you
you inside of me
i would use every word in my vocabulary
to spoon feed you strength
breast feed you security
i would do that for you
see i am a poet
but i dont
write
love poems

Jim Morrison

Freeze Tag

One shoeless sole
in front of the other
toes pressing the green blades
into the mud below it.
A baby toothed smile as I'm caught
spun around
and frozen by the touch of a childhood friend
stopping me, motionless.
A statue.
Holding still was worse then tripping up
and skinning a knee
an unmoving youth and an inner child screaming
FOR THE LOVE OF GOD!
WOULD SOMEONE PLEASE UNTAG ME?!
Now I'm older
and freeze tag has been replaced by the game
called life
and an inner child muted by responsibility
yet sometimes still, I feel frozen
when I've run too fast and skinned my knee
one too many times
I, at times, will freeze myself
leave my mind in a waking sleep
still in motion but emotionless
save some strange detached longing
for happiness, fulfillment
a quiet obsession to hear that young voice
buried deep inside
so I hold still
and catch the hint of a whisper
in the inhale exhale of my breath

and better yet, I start to remember
I recall what it was about the game
that I loved
It was the chase
the chase that as I grew older
I became afraid of
How Ironic
that as a boy
I ran to avoid getting frozen
and now I'm frozen
to avoid running
to avoid the embarrassment of tripping up
and skinning a knee
but now I see it was
the feeling of freedom
the fun of trying to outrun whoever is after you
the thrill of touching someone
releasing them when they're struck stiff
so the next time I find I can't move
or be moved
I'll remember what it's like to lose
silently frozen

Chris Murray

target audience

when he comes to your door
with a briefcase and tie
and that tie is tight enough to restrain
but loose enough so he don't die

and he's making fast talking offers with a fork tongue and a Sullivan nod
and what's in the briefcase?
is it a stash of cash and Crockett and Tubbs are hiding around
the corner? or is it full of those Jehovah Witness pamphlets

with the Readers Digest illustrations of happy people who
made the wise and profound decision not to be you
but then he speaks of another glory
the American dream
which somehow seems to have been misconstrued in his mind
into a chain-letter driven scheme of corporate advertising
and he is showing you charts and figures; and if you will just
sign here please, and wear this beeper and accompanying
chip implant and agree to biological research to be
performed on another dimension, then you may already be
the winner of 3 million dollars! and your very own cubicle,
desk and file cabinet to punch in on a military time clock so
you never know how much you've worked, punch out and
have another sleepless night rolling over having a horrifying
dream of your boss naked and flagging a donkey

wake up
cook some food in a device you shouldn't stand within 7 feet
of and drink some water that killed your child's goldfish
but as part of our dominance through denial
you always have the option
of watching "Who's the Boss" weekdays at 7:30pm
see this is the hypnotic post you can revolve around
well the need for security is what we are talking about
isn't it?
and that Tony Danza is a riot!
it really makes you wonder "who is the boss?"
is it the daughter, or the mother, or is it Tony?
a lot of our employees like to pose these sorts of questions
around the water fountain

and this guy, who's dressed to the nines in all the vulgarity of
late 90's dot.com swank; you know the Moby CD in the
beamer, the coke problem, the loft apartment
this guy is reading you straight out of a book
you're vulnerable and at a point in your life where you are
thinking of enrolling in I.T.I.
and taking a course in business management

or sending away for free information on becoming a private
detective; from your own home
cuz even Sally Struthers can sweet talk someone as lost as you
in this world
you've even applied for that credit card offer you received
didn'tya?
knowing full well, when it claimed it was for those who had
"credit problems" that really meant it was for those so
desperate and confused they will helplessly screw themselves so far into debt
that overdosing on Prozac while listening to Neil Diamond's
soundtrack score for "Jonathan Livingston Seagull: the
movie" is unfortunately the most likely outcome

but you're still alive, so you buy the last hip album you knew
which is now in the cutout bin. and then you whine about
how there used to be
arcades and vinyl and an ozone layer
and you hate your cat, cuz your cat is a tired little bitch that
snarls at you when you try to pet her and always has some shit
dangling from her ass
and your eating a sandwich made with "I can't believe it's
not butter" and that's when you realize
you've become
their target audience

why soon you will be drinking Zima in a suburban bar
with a washed up valley girl in matching acid wash jeans and
jacket, and hell its been awhile
so you join her in a psychopathic affair and she'll move in
and send your phone bills through the roof talking about you
on the psychic phone line
and then when she leaves
you've sunk so low you find yourself at a Tony Robbins seminar
where you realize that he has so much self belief that he is possessed
and that giant confident smile is on his face because...
he......is about......to eat you

and it's that same weird flaky smile that the guy at your

doorstep is making right now
groping for your soul, practicing the Art of Deception through
gestures, convincing you of things by making the hand
configurations of the people in Michelangelo's "The Last Supper"
he's doing the neuro-linguistic used car lot trick
yes, I'm talking about subliminals; don't laugh, they're real
I'm talking naked people writhing in fantastic orgy
in a bowl of Cheerios
I'm talking about a penis wearing shades trying to pass as a camel
I'm talking Britney Spears in the "Got Milk" ad
I mean, a nubile girl in a tight outfit with white cream on her lips
how far does it have to go people?!
I suppose you don't even know that all this time
Richard Simmons has been speaking in tongues

so think; is security what you are asking for?
and what kind of question is that?
cuz he's knocking at your door
and most likely he'll get in
and then soon you'll be inanely defending with some
newfound unbreakable subconscious loyalty to the W.W.F.
that the wrestlers are really hitting each other
or, "oh, my Baker's card is saving me so much money; blah, blah, blah, blah"
and then as your shaving or putting on the layers of make-up
you hesitate and see yourself in the mirror
and you can see it for just a moment
and oh, God
you've become
their target audience

the greyhound

and now, the airports are half empty
Americans are afraid to fly
but i can just imagine the horror on their faces
as they first experience the world
of THE GREYHOUND

constant over booking, missed transfers in the middle of the
night, sleeping sitting up wedged up against the retired used
car salesman who's been drinking Old Crow all day and
mumbling "i never meant to hurt her" over and over as the
teenage mini version of Eminem from Des Moines keeps kickin
the back of your seat
and a haggard family of seven is arguing up front in trailer park slang
cuz Uncle Willy's been touching Joanna again

as night falls some hippie girl pulls out her guitar and wails like
a cat in heat an unbridled rendition of "moon shadow"
which everyone tries to ignore and its making us all blink a lot
and just stare out at the endless chains of fast food strip malls
& gas stations like sad caged fish
and then the toiletry door at the back of the bus opens and
oh no, it's grampa again who's walking out bug eyed & dizzy
from gettin his skinny ass thrown all around back there on the can
and then of course there's me, sitting across from you; and
guess what? I've got crabs

no, i bet the Greyhounds aren't much busier
no one who's too cautious to fly because of the chance of
another terrorist takeover is going to want to live through the
hell that is absolute & routine on a bus trip of any significant distance

i once went from Albany to Omaha pressed up against the window by a 350lb
woman
we didn't exchange any words and i made a series of facial
expressions that conveyed i wasn't even aware of anything unusual
i was just happy the gregarious militia member with an
insatiable need for approval got off in Philadelphia
and then there was the ride to California with a hessian on
mushrooms i believe may have been channeling coyote
singing Black Sabbath songs in an eerie falsetto voice and
reciting Nostradamus quatrains
and all through the night had me spellbinded with a hypnotic
mystical stream of consciousness rant that went on for hours
about U.F.O's & how Jim Morrison really died and ended with:

"i don't know who God is, but he's crazy as a madman, and
he's runnin the whole thing…he controls it all…ha ha ha ha ha!!"

out there
runnin through the prairies
deserts & mountain
like thieves
passing refineries, compounds & production factories
at 65 mph
going by unnoticed escaping the grasp of industry
& its menial plan for our lives

speeding past each new town
belonging nowhere and to no one
unclaimed by each city and its harsh realities that imprison men
we are free as long as we are moving
fleeing the routines that had starved us and made us beg for shelter
on a pilgrimage full of last chances and last minute decisions
with desperate dreams that require discount rates
pursuing new lives with what was left of our past
stuffed in suitcases and duffle bags

my Momma

my mom just got back home from swindling a free bottle of
water by way of a brief stop at some church; she walks in the
door complaining about the bible they gave her along with the water
I am in her house that is a museum of strange artifacts
thousands of baskets lurking everywhere
hung on walls
next to a "bunny as large cow" painting
wandering hobo clown figurines
and a creepy display case filled with a dozen girl dolls that
are locked inside the glass cage and stare out at the living
room with the sad and empty stares of abandoned children

the cat; who is absolutely schizophrenic (and is the latest in a

long line of pets that no on in the family paid any attention to)
conducts a possessed unnerving look hidden among the
dozens of small decorative pillows that are arranged on the
sofa; the cat has yet to be named

there's a small stuffed animal of the gremlin Gizmo, that has
been hanging on the wall for the last fifteen years and she
herself has no idea why...
I offer to throw it out, but apparently she has plans for this toy
this is no one to argue with
this is a woman who will haggle at a supermarket and win!
she's known by name at every customer service department in town
in the check-out aisle, she's the one holding up the line
reviewing the receipt as if it were the lost dead sea scrolls
to be slowly inspected with reverent intonations

this is the one who will buy a BBQ pit for $40 she doesn't really
have because its original price was $80 and even though
she'll never use the pit and knows it; she's absolutely giddy
and beside herself at the savings she secured; soon it will find
its place in the basement where it's rumored there's a pool
table, although no one can find it

but she's standing; albeit with some new tangled perm, chain
smoking, and eyes bulging out that tell the story of a single
woman raising a family on nothing but muster
driving her three despondent children through cold
snowstorms in a hand me down Gremlin with the muffler
scraping the icy ground, til we got home to a small apartment
in downtown known as "crack alley"

and year after year
ma worked and worked and worked
struggling, chasing cockroaches away from the dishes before
commencing on another sleep deprived and maniacal fit of
"macaroni and cheese surprise"
she finally got a hold and drug us up out of poverty
and eventually to a full-sized house

which burnt down, and then losing everything
we lived in a shelter, then an apartment again and then a house
because she worked as hard as any man
because she never gave in
because she has a heart that's as powerful and stubborn as a
mammoths plodding across the Arctic; because of her,
the family survived

Zedeka Poindexter

Incense

It's a strange thing when you loose your faith in God
Loose the certainty of prayer
It's lonely
Confusing
Because you remember yourself being independent, proactive and responsible
Someone told me God helps those who help themselves and I took that to heart
In the process began taking on responsibility for people and situations
outside my realm of control or understanding
Took on burdens that were beyond me
Instead of the world on my shoulder
It was in my chest making me labor to take a deep breath
It was in my throat making me work to swallow
And it was in my heart making me hurt for futile reasons and bleed at random
I could feel it holding me
And the once animated soul could do nothing but sit still silent and crying
Watching my tethers to reality snapping from the pressure
Wishing for solace
Not knowing where to find it
Just knowing that it—something
Had to come for me
Before I threw myself willingly over the edge
What came was my sister
Saying in a calm voice light Incense and pray
I couldn't

Didn't remember the abandon
Didn't' remember how to let go of the things that weren't mine
She got me off that ledge to the center of my bed
Walked me through the things that I needed
Darkness, incense, fire
Had me think through the realm of my understanding
Let me go as I got to the point of reality being visible but not quite mine
Focused on the flame
Checked my breathing
And then the prayers came
Real ones
Not demanding or explaining
Just release
As I found my prayers to be their own answer I started over
Sent my rough hewn, barely conscious psalms on scented smoke and watched
them return as the will to heal myself, the
    power to sever unnecessary ties and the understanding that I am not the
one in control
When the Incense burned out and there was no more smoke to send my psalms
on
Not OK
I was not healed
Not perfect
But ready

Learning Lullabies

I started to learn Spanish a year ago
Not as part of a conscious effort
But because it was part of my husband
Who he is
And I'm not fluent, but I know just enough
Just enough to understand his terms of endearment
Because they are so much sweeter natural and untranslated
Hearing things like that seduced me from the beginning
As they do now
And we have a baby coming

I am lucky enough to hold the beginnings of a child with brilliant brown
eyes like it's father
And I want those eyes to see parents that do everything in their power to
understand each other
Respect each other
Love each other
And that involves a lot more than language, but language is a start
So when he started to sing Spanish lullabies into my belly
I learned them
Rotated those songs with the spirituals I was raised on
So even in the womb, our baby know balance
Learns it the way I did
The way only love can teach you
By seeing the different paths and pasts that are our family
And all of them supporting me on my own way
I want my children to know their rosaries and how to pray to La Virgin
Just as they know the primitive power of tent revival speaking in tongues
I want my children to see their parents dance together
Laugh, kiss and belt out Aretha Franklin and Celia Cruz
Because the same way my husband and I found we needed to integrate our
lives to be happy
Our children will have to integrate what their parents are to be complete
Because I'm not raising fragmented adults
That know nothing more of multicultural than a census box
Current media pseudo acceptance of different shades of brown
Or the fact beer companies sponsor black history month adds and get
magically conscious on Cinco de Mayo
We are, as our children will be, more than that
And maybe I didn't take enough time to find out why before
But now both of us have to become more that what we are
Because there will be children involved
So I will start with the basics
Live my life with the passion this love inspires
Love my man with the reverence that matches the prayer God answered when we
met
Raise our children for the day they will leave home and make me proud
And for tonight
Learn the words of Spanish lullabies my husband sings into my belly

Terry lee Schifferns

Love Poem

Hey baby, just don't be expecting to hear me say I love you
cause love carries all that negative connotative kinda historical crap;
like the day your cat died
when she or he or wait was that me who left?
Packed it all up and was gone, so gone, long gone, gone again, all gone,
gone-gone, gone for good god damn it this time—
or when they felt that way and I didn't
or worse yet, when I felt that way and they didn't
kind of love stuff
and then there's the push & pull,
c'mere—no—go away love blush
or the I'll say it if you say it,
but you have to say it first
game time, what time?
Night time kind of blues lovin' rubbish.
Then there's always the first, or the best,
and who can forget the worst, or the last,
and what about the old grew cold kind of love mush.
But I want the new, not used kind of love, thank you.
No lost time in a sleazy motel
for a one night stand
when you prayed the next day
the slurred word didn't slip out past numb tongue,
you know—the ilovu word—
the old ball and chain,
down the drain,
you're always gone,
look what you made me do
mine mine mine kind of love.
Then there's the—after all I done for you
U O Me, I O U

paid in full & no withdrawals, deposits only, please
Love &Trust you can bank on it kind of love.
Hey, I'm not looking for an insurance policy with a one year warrantee
against breakage and I don't guarantee against forever.
And who said anything about forever, anyway?
Who needs the—I do, really I do, honest, I do
but I need breathing space
and right now I gotta run
so how about I call you next week kind of love rush.
No surreal, movie myth, here and gone, love fluff for me.

I don't want no heavy as gold, every night for fifty years
monogamous monotone love crud.
I mean love could mean anything;
it's what old ladies say to pug faced dogs
and anyway that's how I feel about chocolate.
So forget the mumbo gumbo of romantic lingo
because I prefer limbo
light as a stone, heart geared low, the shaking quiver
of slipping in and out like a radio turned low on a stormy night kind of
love.
So lets skip the shades and curtains of all that love junk and I'll just say,
hey baby,
I kinda like you.

To the Man with the Ruby Mars Heart

You, yes, you
the man with the Ruby Mars Heart
I have something secret and sweet
like chocolate, but not
You want?
I want you to want...
You, dreamer of Mountains
You, gazer of Stars
You do so much me please
And please me so much

I fall and I fall and I fall again
I fall right into your Ruby Mars den
Den of delight
Den of yen
Let's make a ruckus
Let's call Love in
You, dreamer of Mountains
You, gazer of Stars
You, Papa Man
with the Ruby Mars Heart
I have something you like
It's secret. It's sweet
like chocolate, but not.
You want?
Do, please.

Jen Shafer

5th Letter to my Father

Dear Dad
I've fallen in love
And I know
That as you read these words
You're scoffing about how an 18-year-old can't possibly know what love is
While simultaneously wondering who the dirty, rotten scoundrel is that has stolen my heart
I need to tell you that it's not just some man
Or some woman

But many

I know them better than I know myself
Because we are real and honest with each other
Which is something I can't often be with myself

And what more could we ask for in a relationship
Because God knows it's never happened between us
At least until tonight

I'd never really been in love before either
But when I walked in for the very first time and saw Matt Mason up on the plat-
form
Talking about Jesus eating M&Ms and babies eating Cincinnati
I felt the same way Matt must have felt when he first laid eyes on Sarah
Because, Dad, I fell in love
Fell like a boulder from the top of the Eiffel Tower
I fell hard
And now I'm broken without them

I can't go two full moons without Johnmark's hair
Or the Golden Monkey
(But who would really want to?)
Because the splendor and tenderness that accompany them
Sustain my soul
Like a root sustains a tree
Phone calls sustain a long-distance relationship
And oxygen sustains all of Earth's human population
I need them

I need Katie F-S's advice on haircuts
And hairs cut
And Zedeka to tell me why to get hands tattooed on my hips
And lips on my breast
I need Dan to hold my hand as we run screaming from Wal-Mart's clutches
And into Target to buy
Passion fruit and oranges
I need Sarah and Sara Lihz to remind me that being a woman is a good thing

Even if it means being a woman in love

Because women are beautiful
I am beautiful, Dad, and even though you may not see that now
They do

This is why I fell in love with a group, with an idea, with a culture
With a promise of love in return
Just for being me

Dad, they have taught me how to love and how to let myself be loved in return
And some of them don't even know my name
You know my name
You know that sometimes I don't have time to talk on the phone, and that when
I do, sometimes I hang up anyway
You know that I'm in love, Dad
In love with Matt and Sarah
Sara Lihz, Dan, and Johnmark

But, Dad
I need you to love me
And Dad,
I need you to know that I love you, too.

Timothy Siragusa

Diablo Luna

They said it's just the lifestyle catching up with
him.
On a good night this place is the center of the.
Mr. Avaricious Teabag, my cousin twice removed,
danced with his wife in the middle of the.
I know a man and he. Of the. With what on the side.
O Hell,
This is what I'm doing
Why I'm doing it and howsoever.
C jumped up on the chair and shouted out,
"Jackie Chan!"
All winsome like and the last band of the night.
Where it all gets weird, dancing winsome-like, is when
we look at the clause regarding Saturday delivery

unless he's all up in that which he begat before.
And that was Iowa. So call him back and get the
spread, with little squiggles all along the corners
and talk trash.
Talk trash all up in the.
Talk trash and they know it.
Talk sanctimonious, self-involved, purblind trash like
it was Mount, Sermon on the.
You gots it.
Now upchuck all you own.
Belike they words was they stars and they babies
asleep in the backseat.
Make like joyous.
Make like you don't know about it.
Make like all you hear is you own beats, feets, and X
all under the bed where y'all's Mama forgot to dust.

Don't be afraid nobody's gonna get elected 'cos of
you.
You done your bit by staying home.

Mitch Tracy

Translation

Today more than 100,000 people filled the Plaza del Sol and the surrounding
streets to protest the impending U.S.-led war in Iraq....The streets were so full
that many storeowners complained that the crowds were using the stores to pass
back and forth between the plaza and the streets surrounding, shouting slogans
and leaving trash and clutter in the aisles.
—*translated from* El País, 15 marzo 2003

We are haunched on the third floor of this bookstore
the crowd is passing
through the lobby like a roaring river.
But we are alone up here,

in the fragile armistice of our own war.
I am translating Pablo Neruda for you,
I am trying to find only the saddest poems.
I am translating the saddest lines
and hope you understand
because it always loses a little in the translation.
I hope you understand
that it is Neruda who is translating me
that my soul is not content to have lost you
that the stars shivering blue in the distance
are shuddering really, sobbing.
The wind that whirls in the night and sings,
sings a song that is old and sad and slow.
I am translating Neruda for you.
He is translating me
and my soul is not content to have lost you.
I loved you and sometimes, sometime, baby
you loved me.

I am translating Neruda and he is translating me.
In nights just like this one
the same dumb paper moon
blanched the same trees silver
and I held you in my arms
and kissed you countless times.
Perhaps, these lilies,
these metaphysics of poppies and birds
these glimpses of shadow and fire
will turn the corners of your mouth
crinkle your skin like paper
bleach you whiter than trash
because Neruda is translating us
and I am trying
but it always loses a bit in my translation.
I cannot translate the war between us,
how you were my country, my home
and I am in exile, crouched on the floor
in this bookstore.

I cannot translate my soul here and now.
I cannot translate Neruda to you
nor the crowd below us chanting
"no to the war" and all the signs and banners
and the Spanish-inflected chorus singing
"Imagine" in the streets outside,
but they are translating me.

—*for sam*

A Song For Jenny

She told me I should be tested.
My blood was drawn four times,
filled three test tubes
and one plastic capillary,
then sent to men in white coats who finished
their lunches, yawned and snapped on gloves
to open the red plastic box
marked biohazard,
the symbol below,
spines and broken circles.

They sent me a printout
in faded blue dot-matrix
all results negative
and crisply printed on glossy paper,
a pamphlet with their logo
about safer behavior.

I told her I was all right,
and in the brittle noise
of long distance static
she sounded like an echo
mourning an echo.

And it's not that she was looking

for someone to blame,
or a point from which to measure her life
to befores and afters.

Years ago, my little brother and I had
chicken pox,
it was a comfort to look at him
and know
that just like me,
he was spotted and marked.

I was not alone;
It is not the same.

But it *was* the same
that he and I were not so strange to each other.
Calamine baths
and night-twisting between sheets for sleep,
we were together,
being siblings of the same disease.

One night, too drunk to play my guitar,
I promised Jenny I would write
a song for her sometime.

But there is no rhythm to reconcile us,
her smell of sandalwood and musk,
and my sterile breath, whiskey and smoke.
Still trying to write a song for us,
I am stuck on the last line,
trying to rhyme sex and death.

Dedication

This is a poem for the wind
that blows in through the cracks
and chills us

makes you hang on for love or warmth

This is a poem for the melting snow
and adulterers in the cold
for the mud caked in my soles
for my sloppy lane you'll have to drive through

This is a poem for you
This is a poem for me
or a song for the end of winter
or a hard long look
at the night sky,
a shout,
a prayer,
a cry out at the moon
waning over the pines.

—for sarah

978-0-595-36297-4
0-595-36297-4

43271638R00085

Made in the USA
Lexington, KY
26 July 2015